For
Calum + Hetty

FLEUR

[signature]

D1334855

Moera Di   8th Oct 2017

FLEUR

THE LIFE AND TIMES OF PIONEERING RESTAURATEUR FLEUR SULLIVAN

With Nathalie Brown

New photography by
Aaron McLean

RANDOM HOUSE
NEW ZEALAND

A RANDOM HOUSE BOOK published by
Random House New Zealand
18 Poland Road, Glenfield, Auckland, New Zealand

For more information about our titles go to
www.randomhouse.co.nz

A catalogue record for this book is available
from the National Library of New Zealand

Random House New Zealand is part of the
Random House Group

New York   London   Sydney   Auckland
Delhi   Johannesburg

First published 2011
© 2011 text, Fleur Sullivan; images from Fleur
Sullivan family collection unless otherwise
credited on page 261.

James K Baxter quotes on page 149: 'Pig Island
Letters, 9' from the Collected Poems of James K.
Baxter, ed. J.E. Weir, p.282; 'Concrete Grady's Death'
from The London Magazine, Vol 4, 1965, p.63.
Reproduced courtesy The Estate of James K. Baxter.

The moral rights of the author have been asserted

ISBN 978 1 86979 552 8

If you have any enquiries regarding any of the
images published in this book please contact
editor@randomhouse.co.nz

Design: www.areadesign.co.nz
Cover photographs: Aaron McLean
Printed in China by RR Donnelley Asia printing Solutions Limited

Pages 2–3: Fisherman's wharf, Moeraki, with
Fleurs Place in the background.
Pages 168–169: Kaik One, Moeraki.
Page 259: The view from the back door of the
kitchen at the Loan & Merc, Oamaru.

CONTENTS

**TO MY CHILDREN,
AND MY FRIENDS – THEY'LL
KNOW WHO THEY ARE.**

'Would you tell me, please, which
way I ought to go from here?'
'That depends a good deal on where
you want to get to,' said the cat.
'I don't much care where,' said Alice.
'Then it doesn't much matter which
way you go,' said the cat.
'So long as I get *somewhere*,'
Alice added as an explanation.
'Oh, you're sure to do that,' said the cat.

Alice's Adventures in Wonderland
LEWIS CARROLL

YOU COULD SAY
I HAD AN IDYLLIC
CHILDHOOD. I WAS
BORN FLEUR DE LYSE
ROSS HENRY ON
16 MARCH 1939.
IF I HAD BEEN BORN
ONE DAY LATER ON
ST PATRICK'S DAY,
MY IRISH-DESCENDED
PARENTS WOULD HAVE
NAMED ME PAT.
SOMEHOW I DON'T
THINK MY LIFE WOULD
HAVE BEEN QUITE THE
SAME IF I HAD BEEN
CALLED PAT.

1

FLEUR DE LYSE

In our house the hunting, gathering, growing and harvesting of food, the pickling, drying and bottling of food, the cooking, presenting and serving of food, were central to our lives. All our important family conversations took place around the dinner table.

While I was still a schoolgirl I began buying gorgeous old domestic antiques and kitchenware. These experiences defined my life as a restaurateur and I've become recognised as much for the ambience I create as for the food I serve.

My family lived on my grandparents' farm at Tawai on the Waitaki River, about 32 kilometres northwest of Oamaru, until I was about five years old. Eight individuals across three generations lived in the house — actually, it was more like four generations because my grandfather was 20 years older than my grandmother. The age difference was because there was no one his age to marry. He was the youngest of 13 children and because he was deemed to be delicate some of his brothers and sisters came to look after him when he married my grandma.

The house was a simple four-bedroom weatherboard place, which was not big enough to accommodate all those Henrys. My great-uncles, Mick and George — we called him Uncle Goog — spent their nights in austere one-room sleepouts, each with high ceilings and tongue-and-groove walls. We had two long-drops for the convenience of the extended family. Great-aunts Bunny and Ettie never married

Robert Percival
Henry — Grandad.

My Aunty Bunny
is in the darker
clothes and Aunty
Ettie in the
beautiful blouse.

and so spent their lives caring for other members of the family. I
remember Aunty Bunny best because she spent all her time at the
farm and besides looking after flocks of turkeys she also looked after
me — she was *my* aunty. She was tall and thin and had pale,
translucent skin. Like a very tall Mary Poppins, she wore her grey hair
tied in a wee wispy knot on the top of her head, which she then covered
with a shiny black straw hat. Aunty Ettie was shorter and more robust
than Bunny. She did lots of baking for the family and was often away
helping out in the homes of some of the other sisters and brothers.

My grandfather had lost most of his property during the
Depression, so his farm was just a small block where he fattened

ABOVE LEFT

Uncle Goog
at the farm.

ABOVE RIGHT

My beautiful
mother with me
in the pram.

RIGHT

Mum — Nora Irene
('Noreen') Ross,
aged five.

ABOVE

With Mum and Dad.

TOP & LEFT

How lucky I am to
have these snaps.

sheep. I had a creek to explore, poultry to tend and ponies to play with. Eventually my younger brother and sister, Gerard and Swea, were added to the tribe.

My brother was about 10 years old when Grandad told him that because he was the boy he would inherit the farm when he grew up. This seemed quite normal to my sister and me. When our great-aunts gave us children an orange or an apple the top would be sliced off for my sister, the side sliced off for me, and my brother would be given the rest. We would get him outside, take it off him and I would divide it evenly among us. Sometimes he was given a glass of beer; we never were.

My father, Bill Henry, and his brother were drovers who brought sheep from all over Otago to my grandad's farm where they fattened them before they were sold. During the war Dad was manpowered to the woollen mills in Oamaru where he worked as a wool classer. He had a second job too, delivering coal at night. When he filled out the census he'd put down his occupation as 'wool scourer' and his religion as 'atheist'. Mum, whose name was Noreen, would get really wild with him because being a wool scourer was not as impressive as being a wool classer. And as for being an atheist! That would really get her mad. He wanted to improve himself so Mum bought him a huge dictionary and he read it every night to increase his vocabulary.

Several of my grandfather's brothers lived on the road that led to Tawai School, where I had the first year or so of my schooling. No one in the family moved too far away.

My grandparents were like Jack Spratt and his wife: my grandma ate the fat and Grandad ate the lean. Grandma's name was Julia but the children all called her Doodie. Grandad and his family were tall, thin people from Northern Ireland whereas Doodie was short and wiry and had a disposition that my grandad called 'bog Irish'. They fought like mad but he never wanted to argue as much as she did. Doodie was fiery and she ran the show. Grandad would just say, 'You'd know, Julia. You'd know,' and that made her really mad. The whole atmosphere at home in the early days was boisterous and lots of fun.

❖

My grandparents taught me the meaning of hospitality. It didn't matter how many or who came to visit, they were always welcomed and fed. My mother was hospitable too, but in a more reserved way. She'd never say 'come to the table' to unexpected guests. She would have invited five people for a meal and that would be it; if someone else came to the door they wouldn't be invited in. In contrast, my grandparents welcomed everyone in and the food was abundant.

Our meals were cooked on the coal range in the tiny scullery at the back of my grandparents' house; every day we would race around gathering bark off the blue gums to fuel the fire. Across the yard from the scullery, under two huge plum trees, was a long wooden building with three doors. Behind one door was the pantry with its shelves of bottled fruit and flour bins, the next one led into the laundry with its big copper, concrete tubs, home-made bars of soap and blue bags, and behind the third door were the stacks of wood and coal.

We ate and relaxed in the room next to the scullery. It had a small fireplace and a big, brightly polished mirror above the mantelpiece, which was covered in a lace-edged cloth and cluttered with ornaments. There was another room reserved solely for eating Christmas dinner.

Looking back, I can see that we ate exceptionally well throughout my childhood. Food and its preparation were central to the lives of the adults around me. It wasn't something I thought of as unusual; we never went to other kids' houses for tea so I had nothing to compare it to.

The adults kept a big poultry run and an ample vegetable garden with fruit trees and bushes of berries and currants. As children we were never squeamish about where our food came from. Rabbits were shot; chickens' and turkeys' heads were cut off. Turkey wasn't just a Christmas treat, it was everyday food. Dad caught salmon and trout regularly and we children caught freshwater lobsters out of the creek and boiled them on the bank together with the eggs we'd sneak out of the henhouse.

I still remember all the wonderful smells from the cooking and the meals. The food we had was plain and plentiful. My grandmother cooked eggs, bacon and chops for breakfast, or sometimes porridge with brown sugar and a blob of butter in

Me, Mum and Swea at Ardgowan Rodeo. Gerard
rode a bucking sheep and I rode, in my new
frock (the frill was to hide my developing bust
and to make me more of a young lady), a huge
draughthorse in the DR horse race.

Parade in Oamaru at the end of World War Two.
Mum is standing behind the P & T sign. Gerard is
seated to the right of the sign and I am seated to his
right. Our faces were blackened with black cork.

Grandad and Doodie's Christmas
present, 1959. From left: Swea,
Gerard and me.

the middle. Aunty Bubs, Dad's sister, who married a Scotsman, put lots of salt in her porridge but no butter and sugar; it was a surprise to learn that other people made porridge in different ways.

Lunch would be cold meat, lots of bread, chutneys and Doodie's lovely cauliflower-based chow chow pickle. For dinner we had generous servings of meat on a big plate with lots of cabbage, mashed potatoes and gravy. However, no one stayed up after the meal to socialise; we all went to bed at about half-past seven. My grandmother and the great-aunts did the dishes and the men went out the back to sleep. It was only later that I learned that other families played cards together or listened to the radio in the evening.

In contrast, Christmas Day at the farm was all about conviviality, hospitality and abundance. All the aunts and uncles came to us and it was the one day of the year when we ate in the proper dining room at the front of the house, rather than in the living room at the kitchen table. There was a Pears Soap print in a long oak frame on the wall in the front room — the one showing a man holding a diamond ring in a box as he proposes to a woman. When I was little I thought he was standing there with his false teeth in his hand.

The Christmas fare wasn't too different to what we usually ate; there was just a lot more of it. Pudding was the exception — huge servings of rich trifle and Christmas pudding laced with threepenny and sixpenny coins. During the rest of the year our desserts were more modest bread or rice puddings and fruit.

The Christmas dinner table was covered with a piece of green plush fabric so the table wouldn't be scratched, with the tablecloth over the top and the salt and pepper shakers in the big round cruet set in the middle. After the meal everyone lay around, groaning.

Every year Aunty Bubs, Dad's only sister, would bring a different child from an orphanage to share Christmas dinner with our family. The poor child could never stomach the rich food and was inevitably sick; this made me think about what other people had or didn't have.

❖

By the time I was six there were too many of us to stay with Grandad and Doodie so my parents took my brother, sister and me to our new home at 58 Orwell Street in Oamaru.

At pony club (far left) with my cousin Zaria
MacGregor (far right). I always had a strong-willed
horse or one that kicked so I had to keep my
distance from the other horses.

Orwell Street is very long and steep, running up one side of
a hill and down the other. We lived right on the crest of the hill
overlooking Waitaki Girls' High School; in the distance we had a
view of the Oamaru Harbour and breakwater, and then of the sea
right out to the horizon.

We kept hens and roosters in a big garden with amazing old
apple and apricot trees, and we children went to pony club and
learnt to ride the ponies we kept in the back paddock. Dad was a
wonderful gardener; he grew anything and everything. He saved
the seeds from his runner beans and broad beans for the next
growing season and he swapped vegetables with the neighbours.

In the paddock where we kept the ponies, Dad had an area where
he grew flowers in rows like vegetables: bearded irises, tulips and
daffodils, whatever was in season. It used to drive Mum mad that
he grew flowers in the paddock just because he liked them but said
he couldn't be bothered fiddling about in her border garden beds.

We still went out to the farm most weekends and for all Christmas
and school holidays. Whenever the grandparents and the great-aunts

and uncles came to town the ladies carried feltex bags, appliquéd with forests of foxgloves, full of eggs and butter, which they sold to the grocers.

I suppose I've always been enchanted by the way other people prepare and cook food. When we first arrived in Oamaru I went to St Joseph's School. I would stand for ages at the convent's kitchen double doors, watching the nuns rolling out and plumping up dough at a huge table. To this day I have vivid memories of them in their aprons with their skirts tucked up into their wide black belts, their ampleness and the flour on the table while they made the bread. But as much as I loved watching the nuns baking, I couldn't cope with the way they punished children who made mistakes in their schoolwork. The errors would be marked with big red crosses and the pages pinned to the back of the kids' cardigans; they would be sent out into the playground for the other kids to jeer at. I wouldn't do any work because I was so afraid I'd get it wrong and after a while I began to refuse to go to school. One day, when my mother had to drag me there, she saw how genuinely terrified I was as I wedged myself in the doorway like a starfish, wailing and crying while she pushed me and a nun pulled me. By this time I was so distraught that my mother pulled me back towards her and decided to remove me from St Joseph's. I then went to Oamaru North School where I was put up a class, which meant I was a year younger than the other kids. That was a mistake on the part of the new school because I never caught up with that lost year of arithmetic, and I have struggled with times tables all my life.

In those days there was a very strong Catholic–Protestant antipathy in the community. Primary school children acted this out by chanting insulting rhymes at the kids from the other schools. I switched from chanting

Proddy dog
sitting on a well
along came the devil
and pushed him into hell

to

Catholic dogs
stink like frogs
in their mother's bathing togs

I felt no loyalty to my former schoolmates, just the need to survive in my new environment.

Kuini Elizabeth Te Maiharoa was a friend at Oamaru North School; years later I came to know her extended family at Moeraki when I met her brother, Michael. I buy my fish from her nephew Gavin Te Maiharoa. Playing at Kuini's house after school while her mother was cooking tea made me realise that other families ate food that was different to what we had at home. The smell of their cooking made me think, That must be what Maori people have for tea. Back then you wouldn't be invited to another child's house for tea; you went home for tea. And you didn't go and stay overnight with other kids either.

My biggest thrill, when I was about 10 years old, was going out to the farm on weekends and being allowed to drive the car at night up the shingle roads around the Waitaki River with Dad crouched on the running board, leaning on the mudguard, shooting rabbits.

I never went deer shooting with Dad but my brother Gerard did. There were no four-wheel-drives back then so they carried out the back straps, legs and the hearts; Dad would hang up the meat to age and slice off any maggoty bits later. We were never wary of anything we were offered to eat. We trusted that if Mum and Dad said it was OK, we could eat it.

I always loved the way my mother presented anything she put on the table, whether it was morning tea or the evening meal. She had a grand sense of style and made everything look beautiful but — she's dead now, so I can say it — the food wasn't always cooked as well as Doodie's. If you dropped one of her scones on your foot you'd be likely to break a bone. Still, the intention was there; Mum would have the food — whatever it was — on a beautiful plate and you'd sit up straight and have good table manners. She always kept an elegant table with a beautifully laundered tablecloth, starched and pressed serviettes, side plates, good cutlery and butter on a dish. Everything was done properly. If we had the fire going during Sunday tea she might have prepared the tea wagon; it would have cheese with a proper cheese knife, boiled eggs with parsley and chives, and the bread would always be buttered. I'd sit there thinking, Oh, this is lovely, because it was always done so elegantly.

Many years later when I first opened Olivers, my restaurant in Clyde, adult customers would sit at the table and wouldn't know what cutlery to use. I found that really odd. I'd think, How did they get to be an adult without knowing that? I still meet young people who come to the restaurant at Moeraki and who first ate at Olivers 20 years ago, and they say to me if they hadn't gone to Olivers when they were young, even if it was only once or twice, they would never have known what to do when they ate out. Our society has now had two or more generations of people who are used to eating their meals on their laps in front of the television.

Like most people at the time my mother cooked on a coal range and she fed us well but economically. For breakfast she often made bread and milk with sultanas or maybe some jam in it. She also made japonica jelly and all those old-fashioned preserves. She even made soap.

If we came home from school for lunch she would make a rarebit or soup; for dinner we had stews and offal. I realised later that offal was considered poor people's food but I loved tripe — still do. We also gathered pipis and cockles from the beach at Friendly Bay and steamed them. Our everyday food, cooked long and slow, was not expensive; Mum liked to save her money to spend on good furniture. You could say I'm very much my mother's daughter.

Mum didn't let me cook or work in the kitchen because she didn't like a mess but she encouraged me to make pot-pourri, which I'd put it in pretty bowls in the living room and bedrooms.

Our neighbours, the Hannans, had a framed photograph of Michael Joseph Savage above their coal range. Mrs Hannan made homebrew in a big barrel and Mr Hannan drank it. I remember one day, when I was quite young, helping Mrs Hannan do the washing and I washed Mr Hannan's socks in the homebrew because I thought it was the rainwater barrel. I don't believe they even tipped it out.

I loved everything about Oamaru: its cool, dry air; its tiny harbour protected from the Pacific Ocean by a fragile breakwater; the pine plantations on the surrounding uplands; the wide streets unfurling over steep hills lined with oak and flowering cherry;

pretty Arts and Crafts houses and limestone mansions. I loved
the courthouse, the Athenaeum, the post office and bank buildings
at the southern end of Thames Street, with their neoclassical
columns and pilasters, urns and pinnacles, scrolls and wreaths.

My mother often took us to the Oamaru Public Gardens to play
on the swings, slides and roundabouts before we visited the duck
pond with stale crusts of bread in little brown paper bags. We'd
skip through the winding paths, under overhanging trees and past
huge rhododendron bushes with fabulously coloured flowers to
every Oamaru kid's favourite glade where the Wonderland statue
stood. Two London street urchins frozen in bronze, stooped down
from the top of a tree stump above our heads. We'd play a game to
find all the delicate fairies, the shiny little rabbits and mice that
hid among the sculpted tree roots and burrows at their feet. The
statues are still there today.

At other times we'd head to the beach at Friendly Bay for a
picnic; Gerard and I would walk beside Mum while she trundled
Swea in a pushchair piled with towels and picnic food. I remember
walking along Harbour Street on the way to the beach, past the
disued, ornately decorated limestone warehouses and commercial
buildings in the old part of town now called the Historic Precinct.

From the time I was about six, a boy called Noel Allen was my
best friend. It was a friendship that lasted right through to Noel's
death in his early 30s. Noel and his mother would often come with
us on our walks to the gardens and the beach. Noel's father had
been a POW and, for reasons of his own, he didn't come home
from the war straight away. Noel and I waited and waited for him
at the top of the path for days. When he finally did arrive he was a
great disappointment to us because he was always either bad
tempered or completely silent, or at the RSA. We either avoided or
ignored him and carried on. Noel just said to my dad, 'Bill, will
you still be my dad?'

Later, when Noel had a bike, he would double me on the
crossbar down to Harbour and Tyne streets, in the old part of
town. We'd make up stories about the people who lived and
worked in those buildings back in the 1880s, or we'd pretend there
were monsters and murderers lurking in the doorways and scare
ourselves to death before belting out of there.

From left to right:
Me, Gerard, Swea and Noel outside
our playhouse/museum.

On one of these excursions while we were fossicking around
behind an old building, Noel found a heap of discarded clocks
and pieces of broken china that had been burnt in a rubbish fire.
It was pirate's loot, so we took it home and buried it in my dad's
paddock next to the playhouse he'd made for us, and buried our
map of the loot somewhere else. Noel and I turned the playhouse
into a museum with labelled exhibits. We'd search the shoreline for
well-weathered boards, then read books from the library about
ships that had sunk near Oamaru. We'd put the boards on the wall
of our museum with a label to say they were off such-and-such a
ship that was sunk in the harbour or foreshore.

At other times Noel and I used to imagine we were Todd and
Annie, the runaway orphans from *School Friend*, being chased by
the orphanage owner Mr Higgins. We'd run from my place in
Orwell Street all the way along Reservoir Road, down, down, down
the hills and into Casa Nova House in Alt Street. It had been built
in 1861 by the Noble family as the centrepiece of a grand estate
and the current owner, old Mrs McMullan, used to give us snacks
of apples and barley water. Then we'd run all the way home to
Orwell Street again. It was a long way.

If we ran down the hills in the opposite direction, towards the public gardens, we'd go down Old Mill House Road, then through a paddock up into what we called the 'Black Forest'. Janet Frame called it 'the plannies' in her books because it was a pine plantation. It was dark and deliciously scary and there were always dead birds around. We'd count as many birds as we could, trying to work out how they died — and scare ourselves half to death.

Noel and I would collect huhu grubs there, which we'd take home and throw on the top of Mrs Allen's coal range. Once they'd stopped wriggling and sizzling we'd pick them off with a steel knitting needle or a darning needle and crunch into them. I've always thrown myself into eating new and exciting foods like shellfish, grubs and boxthorn berries. There was no way Mum would let us put huhu grubs on her coal range.

From time to time we'd sneak into the junkyard owned by Janet Frame's brother Geordie, on the far side of the Black Forest to see what treasures we could find. Once he gave me a copper kettle, which I've still got, but Mum said that we weren't allowed back there because he was crazy and his sister was in a mental home. Given that we were exceptionally curious kids, this started a whole new line of thought for us, and we never stopped visiting him.

Years later, I read Janet Frame's book *Owls Do Cry* and just loved it because there was so much in it that had the flavour of Oamaru. I rang my mum to share my excitement. She said, 'Yes, I've read it, and there was no need for her to say all those horrible things about people in Oamaru.' That was the end of our conversation about Frame's literature forever! It was a common response from people in the town.

Like most small towns in New Zealand in the 1940s and '50s, Oamaru had its warring gangs of primary-school children. My brother Gerard, Noel and I, together with the Tavendale kids and the Dunlops, held the ground on the side of the hill that was covered by the Black Forest, and the Jimmy Veitch gang battled us from the other side. We were nominally Catholic and the Veitches were Orangemen who flew an orange flag on St Patrick's Day, so Jimmy Veitch was the enemy. Dad always wanted to chop down their flagpole but Mum wouldn't let him.

We all read war comics and immersed ourselves in stories of World War Two. Our gang played in the deep trenches that had been dug for civil defence during the war, pretending we had to hide because the Germans were coming. We'd cover the trenches with sticks and pine needles, and we could crawl quite a long way underground without being seen. Jimmy Veitch and his gang would come whooping over from their side of the hill to smash all our good work, then we had to run the gauntlet to get back home, which was a very serious matter. If we ran in one direction we had to dodge the Jimmy Veitch gang with their sticks; if we ran the other way we'd get to Casa Nova House and the lovely Mrs McMullan, but we'd then have to go the long way home.

Some time ago Jim Veitch turned up to eat at my restaurant in Moeraki. He is now an associate professor at Victoria University, specialising in the study of religious and political conflict! When I saw him I said, 'The Jimmy Veitch gang! In *my* restaurant!' and we roared laughing. He and his wife have come back several times since then and we're always very pleased to see each other.

The mid-1950s brought a charmed teenage life when you were pretty and popular and your mother always made you nice dresses. Mum made me outfits copied from designs I saw in *Seventeen* magazine, which I read every month for years.

When I was at school, Christmas seemed forever away. Growing up was forever away. Going to school had no particular purpose or meaning for me. I never understood that one day I would have to earn my living or that I was ever going to grow up. I guess I was never told.

My father's sister never went to school because Grandad didn't believe that education mattered for girls so, whichever course I did at school, whatever I was doing, I never saw it as relevant to the real world. I wasn't guided towards any particular line of work. I don't ever remember a teacher trying to find out what I particularly liked doing or what field I might like to work in. But looking back I realise that my home life prepared me for the work I eventually took on. The food my family produced, its presentation, the hospitality — these were all lessons that stayed with me.

However, at school my whole focus was on reading novels and studying history and art. I really loved history and I read mainly

Me and Lexie Hamilton
at the Power Board
Picnic — Danseys Pass
Holiday Camp.

At Oamaru
Harbour wearing my
new coat.

At Waitaki River, Kurow.
The red top and black
shorts were copied from
movie stars.

biographies and autobiographies because of their social-history content. I read anything I could find about how people in the past lived their daily lives, what they wore, what they ate and how they struggled.

Years later I visited Olveston in Dunedin, the 35-room mansion built by David Theomin, a successful businessman, at the turn of the twentieth century. It was gifted to the people of Dunedin in 1966 by his daughter, Dorothy. I wasn't particularly interested in imagining the luxury of the genteel diners in the banquet hall or the women sitting in the little side room while they watched the young people dancing. I've always been much more interested in the domestic side of things. In the kitchen I saw what the servants worked with: the coal ranges, the gleaming copper and brass, the scrubbed kauri benches and the butler's pantry where all the good things were lined up in glass cupboards. I was fascinated by the butler's sink and the lead-lined cupboards, the little hatch for the man who delivered the meat, and the laundry with its wooden flap where the chimney came out to take the smoke away from the copper. I could stand looking at that and daydream forever about what they did and who they were and why they worked there. I love it, just love it all.

It was the same interest in our country's early European heritage that led me to think about buying the former Teschemakers Catholic School outside Oamaru when it went up for sale in 2000. I loved the laundry the most: the ironing room with its pure-white scrubbed wooden rails where the nuns hung the sheets, and the scrubbed floors, tables and coppers. I considered the possibility of making goat's cheese there but the practicalities of building fences to contain goats in this market-gardening area was one of the reasons it didn't seem such a good idea. I went out there again 10 years later to take part in a pre-dawn occupation of the beautiful Petre-designed chapel in what tuned out to be a successful attempt to stop the exquisite Italian marble altar from being pulled out and relocated to a 1970s Catholic church in Dunedin. Long story, and it's still going on, but I really believe these precious things should be preserved for future generations to appreciate. I've also been involved in preserving and restoring the historic buildings and goldmining heritage of Central Otago for nearly 30 years.

❖

When I was 14, Mum opened Henry's Grocery Store on the corner of Nen and Thames streets and we shifted into the house at the back of the shop. I got my driver's licence when I was about 15 and from then on we kids would deliver the groceries from the back of a fawn Hudson Terraplane before we went to school or work. I was the driver and my brother or my sister would jump out with the groceries at each house and then run to catch up with me the next time I stopped. Dad helped out with the shop too, but it was Mum's shop and she loved it.

Years before Dad had left the woollen mill and was working at an Oamaru department store called The Polytechnic in the middle of Thames Street that sold household goods, dressmaking patterns and fabrics rolled onto huge bolts. The staff on the ground-floor counters would put the money in a wee metal chute, pull the lever and shoot it up to the office. Dad worked upstairs in the furniture department and sold carpets, curtains and furniture.

Meanwhile Mum did a furniture-upholstery course at Oamaru Polytech. She and Dad used to buy antiques at the auction rooms on Thames Street. They restored the furniture and did deep buttoning, and that's when my obsession for collecting furniture and beautiful old household goods started. I have to call it an obsession because no matter how many demolition doors or linen napkins I have, I can't pass up another. But they've always found a home.

During my last years in school and once I started working I went regularly to the auction in my lunch hour. I'd buy whatever I could afford. The auction was held once a week and I soon had a big collection of old bowls, plates and platters, beautiful old picture frames and rolling pins. I bought a metal apple peeler that spun the apple around while a little blade took the peel off, tin boxes with old postcards in them, bits of clothing, bits of lace. I've probably got New Zealand's biggest collection of old linen! In later years, my bargain-hunting instinct has extended to demolition timber, windows, doors — even staircases and full kauri verandas.

One day when I was still at school I saw this beautiful old wooden highchair in the auction rooms. While I was imagining a little child with curls sitting in it, an elderly man approached me and showed me how it turned into a rocker. He said his family had had one. I think he was about 75, which seemed incredibly old to me at the time. I knew I had to buy it; when I realised it converted into a rocking chair I tried to hide the rocking rails so no one else at the auction would know how special it was. I got it for 12s 6d, which wasn't that cheap in those days. I asked my father for the money and he lent it to me.

While I was in high school I worked at the Excelsior Milk Bar on Sunday afternoons. I earned 10s 6d each weekend, so I was able to pay Dad back over time. The part-time job meant I always had some money of my own to buy more things at the auctions.

I had no idea what I would do when I left school. In the late 1950s, girls like me were expected to get any job to tide them over until they got married. When I was at high school, it seemed to me that what a girl's parents did for a living determined how much education she was given or how much time the teachers would spend on her.

Because I was doing the commercial practice course, when the time came for me to leave school one of my teachers, Miss Nancy Brooker, told me about an office-junior position advertised at the law firm of Lee Grave & Zimmerman, located at the top of the Oamaru Opera House. I dutifully applied, and got the job.

I loved working there and adored Miss Margaret McKay, one of the solicitors. The fact that she paid me attention gave me confidence. Staff had long holidays at Easter and Christmas but as a rule law offices did not pay well. My friend Eunice was working at the Waitaki Electric Power Board and earned £5 a week while I got £2 10s. She told me about a job opening at the power board, but I couldn't bear to leave the law office. Mum and Dad said I had to decide for myself, but Dad said money wasn't everything. So I talked to Miss McKay. I was crying my eyes out when I told her why I wanted to go but that I also didn't want to leave. She said, 'That's all right, my dear. I don't think you have a big future in the law so if you want to work elsewhere and earn much more money, I think you should do that.'

So I took the office junior's job at the power board. I was 17 by then, and Norma Butcher, one of my friends who worked there, and I would bike through the old part of town during our lunch hour to fish from Holmes Wharf. (Life seemed to have come full circle when

I decided to open a new restaurant in the 1882 Loan & Mercantile building at the end of Harbour Street in the Oamaru historic precinct. It felt significant that I was 71 — 17 with the numerals reversed — back in the place where I started.)

When I first started work at the power board I became acutely aware of social interactions in a big workplace. There were lots of people my age and we all got along well. The older staff made a point of getting to know us; they helped us learn how to do our work and made conversation at morning and afternoon tea.

Morning tea was always a big part of life at the power board. As an office junior it was part of my job to collect everyone's money for their orders from Brown's Tea Rooms across the road. The tea rooms had a carpet runner, polished tables and chairs, oak-panelled walls and chrome cake stands. Every day they made yeast buns, sugar buns and pies. One day, after I'd been at the power board for several years, I suddenly looked at my yeast bun, which was the size of a big saucer, and thought, I can't eat another one of those. The more I looked at it the sicker I felt and of course, being a young girl, everyone thought Ah-ha . . . The engineer asked if I was all right and I said, 'I've worked here for four years and I've eaten two yeast buns every day, five days a week.' He worked out that I had eaten the equivalent in yeast buns of the distance between the power board and the Pukeuri freezing works — about 6 kilometres. Everyone laughed like mad and I said, 'No wonder I feel sick.'

I loved having responsibility for buying the food for the afternoon teas when someone retired. Aspro's fish shop was just over the road and in season I'd go there and buy crayfish. I'd then butter slices of white bread and do a fantastic afternoon tea.

At other times the girls and I would cook up some quite good feasts in our staffroom. We boiled eggs in the jug and could even fit a small crayfish into it. (When we did that there'd be a lot of froth coming over the top. There'd also be an incredibly bad smell and the tea would be tainted for a while.) When I look back on my time at the power board it seemed to be all about food and growing up.

When Mum sold the grocer's shop, Gerard, Swea and I stayed with her mother for a while until we were able to join Mum and Dad in the new house. My grandma, whom we called Rossie, had been one of the 'beautiful Foley girls' from Waimate, and now lived near

Waitaki Power Board float, 1956. I am seated at left, with Eleanor Brain and Eunice Houliston on my right. In the background the linesmen are boiling the copper and wringing sheets through a huge mangle.

At a barn dance with Rosemary Thomas and James Smyth. Later on I was their bridesmaid.

the Catholic basilica in Reed Street. Nearly everything she fed us came out of her garden. My brother and sister took their lunch break between midday and one o'clock and mine was between one o'clock and two o'clock. Rossie cooked the meal to be ready for midday; God knows what time she put the cabbage on but when my turn came I got what remained at the bottom of the pot — the stewed cabbage leaves and all these wee baby snails. She'd dish it up on my plate and I'd eat it all because I didn't want to hurt her feelings. The snails actually weren't too bad; they were only the size of a small broad bean and you would just go 'Crunch!' I was probably the only one in the whole town eating snails for lunch.

Oamaru in the late 1950s was not the most exciting place in the world if you were a teenager. When I was about 18, I decided to put a bit of spark into our lives by organising picnics. I invited people from the power board; not just the ones who were my age but also the young married couples and some of the much older staff. I'd get people to bring food and drinks and barbecues and we'd head off to Gemmells Crossing, a lovely bush setting on the banks of the Kakanui River south of the town. I also organised town socials, which passed for sophistication in Oamaru at the time. I chose The Homestead on Holmes Hill for the venue because I liked the feel of the place. It had been built in 1864 as the home of one of the town's early businessmen but was now used as a function centre. After the invitations went out to people from the power board and a few old school friends, I sold tickets to cover the hiring charge and arranged for everyone who had one to bring a guitar and someone else to bring a record player and their rock 'n' roll records.

The girls brought a plate for the supper and sometimes The Homestead did the catering. No alcohol was sold because Oamaru was a prohibition town; it had been dry since 1905 and the alcohol ban wasn't lifted until 1962. In fact, at my 21st birthday party, Dad hadn't ordered enough grog to go around and he had to drive to Georgetown, a half-hour out of town, to get some more.

Being a fairly low-key party girl was pretty much the extent of my wild teenage years. At the age of 21 I did what my teachers had expected and got married.

JIM SULLIVAN
HAD A MODEL A
FORD AND A
JAMES DEAN LOOK;
HE'D FINISHED
HIS ELECTRICIAN'S
APPRENTICESHIP
AND GAVE ME
THE IMPRESSION
HE WASN'T
INTERESTED IN
SPENDING ALL HIS
LIFE IN OAMARU.

2

WEST COAST WIFE

All in all he seemed to be the least boring young man in the town and in 1961 those were grounds for marriage as far as I was concerned. I thought getting married would give me freedom, and I'd have an exciting life. When we announced our engagement Dad said, 'Don't bring her back when you find out she can't cook!' and Mum gave me a quick lesson on how to make pikelets.

Once we were married, we thought we'd live in the North Island for a while. Jim's parents lived in Whataroa on the West Coast — Mr Sullivan was working on a power plant there — so we went over to say goodbye.

Whataroa is the township closest to the white heron sanctuary on the edge of the Okarito Lagoon, about 30 kilometres north of the Franz Josef Glacier. While I was chatting to the local policeman, he told me the brewery was looking for a couple to manage the Okarito Forks Hotel. It sounded like a good idea, and we more or less fell into the job. That was as far south as I travelled on the Coast for quite a long time because I enjoyed managing the pub so much that I had no time to go further south. There was only one road; the Haast Pass hadn't yet opened and there was a lot of traffic on the main road heading to and from the Fox and Franz Joseph glaciers. Travellers would stop at The Forks on the way. It was really funny to watch their faces when I told them I'd never been south of The Forks; I enjoyed omitting to mention that I'd only been there three weeks.

LEFT

Out the back of the
Forks Hotel with
my Dalmatian dog.

BELOW

Friends Faey
Rutherford and Ian
Sutherland at the
Forks Hotel.

The Forks was a long, single-storey wooden building in a
shortened T-shape with a public bar and seven bedrooms. It had
only just had the power put on and it still had a kerosene fridge
and an Aga stove. Coke for heating and cooking was stored in
a shed at the back, along with a big boiler called a donkey that
heated the water. I had to keep both the donkey and the Aga
stoked up with coke all the time if I wanted to have hot water and
a stove hot enough to cook a meal. What's more, I had to go down
the paddock to pump the water up as well. Jim ran the bar and I
did everything else, as far as I remember.

Mr and Mrs Hibbs
at the white heron
sanctuary, Okarito.

It rains all the time on the Coast. If there was an exceptional downpour the sides of the road would collapse and the traffic caught between the slips would have to be rescued. If the stranded motorists were on my patch, they stayed at the pub and I had to feed them. Whenever that happened, we had a full-scale impromptu party. In those days, no alcohol could be served in public places throughout New Zealand after 6 pm. The law had been introduced in 1917 and was in place until 1967 when the hours were extended to 10 pm. But the West Coast was no place to refuse a man a drink at any hour of the day.

When I started at The Forks I had no idea how to cater for working men and paying guests; up to that point I'd cooked only party food. At first I bought huge tins of Watties K brand soup by the crate. I soon made friends with the butcher, Stumpy Thomsen, in Whataroa and asked him, 'What would I buy to make a roast?' He taught me a lot in the next two years.

I remember a lady called Mrs Hibbs who was married to a man who was . . . well, you said 'Negro' in those days. Mr Hibbs was part-Negro; his grandad had jumped ship in Nelson and that's how his family came to be on the Coast. The Hibbses and a wonderful family had run The Forks before I took over, and

Mrs Hibbs was a great help. She taught me how to make real soup with a meaty bone, vegetables and pearl barley. Other good ladies of Whataroa, the sawmillers' wives, showed me how to make basic pub meals: soup, meat, potatoes and vegetables, and desserts. I made bread puddings and rice puddings all out of the Edmonds book that Mum and Dad had sent me off with as a dowry. I think I'll be remembered on the Coast for my Edmonds custard with sultanas.

I couldn't do much with the décor but I kept the whole place clean and shiny. I had ventilation holes put in the linen cupboard and a heater in the bottom to air the sheets because everything on the Coast was damp and smelt of mildew. At the beginning, I'd often wander off and let the Aga go out. After a while I learned not to do that but the stove was very temperamental — if I didn't get it stoked up just right at night it would have died out by morning. Whenever that happened I'd lie a two-bar heater on its back with the element facing upwards. I learnt to fry breakfast for quite a few people on a two-bar heater, but it was fairly nerve-racking, I can tell you.

The Aga looked lovely and it cooked food beautifully but it was terribly hard to light. I'd buy piles of wooden pegs to use as dry kindling because the wood on the Coast was always damp. I'd put the pegs in the middle of the stove, tip petrol on them, stand back and throw matches at it until the pegs were alight. One time it went BOOM and lifted the whole Aga off the ground! It came back down on a funny angle.

The aluminium pots took some getting used to as well. It was a real shock the first morning I checked the stew I'd cooked the night before and left on the bench ready for the next day's lunch, to find a fuzzy grey-green mould coating the meat. I never left food in one of those pots again.

Most of the customers at The Forks were typical Coasters. Sawmilling was the biggest local industry in the 1960s and all the sawmillers were working in the plantations. They would wrap a line around the trunk of a tree to pull the logs to the trucks. Well, those wires can break. It was dangerous work and most of the guys didn't have all their fingers; they were fairly broken and scarred.

Barry Crump drove a tractor in the area at the time; when he

On location with Mike
Bennett, photographer for
the National Film Unit.

published his first book, *A Good Keen Man*, a whole gang of Coasters went up to Wellington with him for the launch. He came back with a pair of blue suede shoes that he wore everywhere until they fell apart.

The people who drank at the pub were mainly roadmen working for the Ministry of Works and tourists. The overnight guests were travellers on their way to or from the glaciers, but there were a few who stayed for a while.

Mike Bennett, who is alive and well on the Coast today, is an Englishman who worked for the National Film Unit in the 1960s. He took photographs for the tourism posters that were displayed in railway stations and bus depots. Mike would stay whenever he had an assignment in the area; he took shots of me looking out over glaciers and standing on lake shores, so I became a poster girl! He stayed on and has since written books on deer culling on the West Coast and the adventures of the venison-recovery guys.

I don't remember a lot of really cold weather on the Coast but one morning when Mike first stayed at The Forks, the pipes froze inside. Mike walked up the passage with a towel wrapped around his waist and his toothbrush in his hand, and in his English accent said that he couldn't clean his teeth because there was no water. I told him to go out and break the ice in a puddle. I couldn't believe that I had to spell this out to him! But that was when he first arrived; he slowly turned into a West Coast bloke.

I came across Mike again when he was the curator of the Arrowtown museum. When he later moved to St Bathans his teenage children and my teenage children met quite independently of us and have remained good friends.

I was fascinated by the roadmen who were the regulars at The Forks. They lived in the bush for the most part but they'd come in for a drink now and then. I'd ask them incessant questions about how they lived. Where were they born? Why had they never married? Why did they live in such solitude?

They were Irishmen who had fought for England in World War One; they couldn't easily go home after the war so they came to the colonies. Most were in their early sixties and they were employed by the Ministry of Works to repair and maintain the road. They didn't have bulldozers, so just chipped away with their picks and shovels, keeping the trenches on either side of the road open so they

The three Black brothers (Ted, Hughie and Harry) built this railway line into the bush to bring their logs out.

Hughie Black's hut. Ian Sutherland is on
the right. Note the West Coast chimney.

wouldn't overflow after the heavy rain. They loaded rocks and
shingle into their wheelbarrows and trundled them away.

The sawmillers invited me into their camps and I sat with them
in their huts. They taught me how to cook in a camp oven where
they made gingernuts and bread, and took me eeling in the bush
creeks. I learned a lot from these men. I remember in particular
the Black brothers, who had put a railway line right into the bush.
They had a tractor which they fitted to the rails; it would go up the
line, right to where they cut the silver pine.

I also remember Michael Moroney, who lived like a troll under
the Whataroa Bridge. He'd made a path of punga logs to his little
house, which had a door and two windows. Outside, on one side of
the hut was a pile of bottles as high as the roof and on the other
side was a pile of rusty tin cans. He'd lined his walls with the pink
pages of the *Weekly News*. Michael could stay in his bed while he
reached over to poke the embers, hang his billy over the fire and
make his cup of tea, and one for me as well.

He had a suit with a black tailcoat and a pure white shirt. I only ever saw him in it twice but it was pristine. He'd been an accountant in a law firm back in Ireland but he said some of the money had stuck to his fingers and that was why he was now in New Zealand tucked away on the Coast.

One of the really notable characters was Patrick Daniel Mullins, who was always known by his full name. He mined the Nine Mile Beach and he'd come out every couple of months with his very rough gold and sell it down at the Whataroa garage. Then, after a few days, he'd come back to The Forks with a roll of bacon, some salt and some flour and he'd be very drunk. He would give me any money he had left, which I'd put on the shelf in the bar and he'd say, 'Tell me when that's gone, girl.' When he'd had enough of civilisation he'd go back to the Nine Mile.

Patrick Daniel Mullins slept standing up; he never lay down unless he was in his hut. He'd just lean against something and go to sleep. He never took his gumboots off either. And he'd won the war, of course. The generals always consulted Patrick Daniel Mullins before they made a move. He had big scars on his face which he'd got during the war; he told me that when he was stationed in the desert he and a few other men got little bugs under their skin which were really painful, so he put some sort of caustic soda on his face to kill them.

There was no escaping him. Sometimes I got sick of his stories and I'd say, 'Look, I've just got to go.' He thought I meant I needed to go to the toilet so he decided I had something wrong with my stomach. He knew quite a lot about bush medicine and brought me a wad of leaves from the bush to chew on to fix me, so that taught me not to muck around with him. I'd just take the leaves and stuff them in my mouth, but not swallow them.

He would walk a few sheep in to the Nine Mile and salt down their meat in seawater to keep him going until he had the urge to come back out. He told me about the way he worked the Nine Mile, fossicking for gold. When the tide was right and the beach 'cut', it revealed the black sand that held very flaky, flat gold and that's what he was waiting for, year after year. He used mercury to separate the gold flakes from the sand and debris. It didn't happen often; he and the other Irishmen who were gold fossickers all dreamed of the next time the beach would cut.

One of the Nolan boys had the beach cut on him once and he didn't have enough equipment or time to get a good haul. For the rest of the time that I knew him he was waiting for the beach to cut again. He was ready but as far as I know it never did.

Being a publican and boarding-house keeper suited me. Every now and then, just for fun, I'd run the hot-water tap when the men were in the showers and they'd be doused with cold water. They'd leap stark naked out of the three little shower cubicles that opened onto the passageway that ran through the hotel. If I had the kitchen door open I could see them hopping around, yelling and running for cover. That was a good trick if I got bored.

One old man who often stayed had the unlikely name of Hink Hornell. He'd be younger than I am now but at the time I thought he was an old man. He wore very thick glasses but they were always broken so he'd Sellotape them up. When he had a shower the Sellotape would get all steamed up and his glasses would fall to bits.

These guys laughed at my lack of experience but appreciated my willingness to learn.

Since getting married, my life had totally changed. I pondered on the fact that when I was single I could go to parties and arrange socials and I was allowed to be pretty and popular. But all of a sudden, two or three weeks after I was married, I was meant to be sensible and able to run a household and a business and produce three meals a day on time. This wasn't easy, especially when I wandered off and the Aga went out while I was underneath the bridge talking to old men.

Jim and I lived and worked at The Forks for about two years and our daughter Kirston was born there. We then moved nearer to Franz Josef Glacier. Jim found work at the sawmill where he learnt to be a saw doctor and we lived in a farm cottage that was powered by a generator.

I felt desperately homesick and lonely. I learnt to smock, knit and sew baby clothes and although I didn't understand the word 'depression', I felt utterly bewildered and isolated living there with this little thing that I truly loved but with no one to show her to.

Kirston, my daughter, at the Franz,
under Mount Elie de Beaumont.

With Kirston at Lake
Mapourika, West Coast.

The lady on the farm down the road was lovely. She would come to visit with her children, one of whom was James Millton, who grew up to start The Millton Vineyard, one of the first organic vineyards in New Zealand. He had a brother and two sisters and they've all been to see me in Moeraki. The children enjoyed visiting me because I had a lawn full of guinea pigs and a Dalmatian dog given to me by Warner Adamson, one of the logging truck drivers.

Our next move was to Westport, where Jim worked as a refrigeration engineer on the boats and I had two more babies, Martin and Brendon. Our time in Westport was probably the saddest time of my whole life, because I was so homesick. Eventually I realised that when you leave your family home it's up to you to make your own home, but it took me a long time to do that.

I could fit all three babies in one of those massive Hyde Park prams; I walked for hours around town looking at the gardens. I became a pretty proficient gatherer of geraniums, pelargoniums and mint because when you're pushing a pram around the town you can pick little bits of the plants you see growing through fences and put them in the pram hood.

I just loved Mrs O'Dea's classic garden with the bricks in a raised zigzag pattern edging the gravel paths. She was an ample, welcoming woman with hard-working hands and she reminded me of my grandparents. We talked over the fence, and when she invited me in I remember stepping over her beautifully scrubbed doorstep and into her kitchen with its scrubbed bench and big wooden table. I thought, Ah, here, I'm in heaven.

Mrs O'Dea had a miniature potager beside her back steps, one of those big oval boilers where she grew chives, parsley and celery. When she saw me looking at it she said, 'Oh, you've got to have some of this one, just go and pick a little bit and put it in your soup. And put that one in your stew.'

It doesn't take much to restore your soul. Just looking at the scrubbed steps, the scrubbed bench and table and the simple little garden, I felt more alive. I used to visit Mrs O'Dea and the butcher and the library ladies — they really saved my life. I survived.

One of the good things about living in towns considered to be economically bereft is finding treasures in second-hand shops. While we were in South Westland all my treasures were in storage

The Doulton Willow Ware teapot
I got in exchange for some of our
wedding presents.

in Oamaru, along with the wedding presents. When we shifted to Westport we unpacked everything and I had all this ugly stuff that people had given us to start our married life. There were horseshoe-shaped chrome fire-iron sets with brooms and pokers and tongs; metal-framed Pyrex casserole dishes in bright colours with tea-light candles in a frame underneath; huge, thick plates made in Japan that broke easily, a collection of the most horrible things you ever saw.

One day we had a magnitude 7.5 earthquake and a big ashet given to me by Doodie when I was very young fell off the mantelpiece above the coal range and broke. I felt like it was just too much to bear.

I knew I needed beautiful things around me so, day after day I put the ugly wedding presents in the pram and took them to the second-hand shop on Westport's main street. I traded them for a blue willow-patterned teapot and a base, which I still have, and a beautiful bamboo lounge suite with crinkly brass detailing, perfect for a sun porch, which included a side table, a corner chair, wee sofas and two armchairs.

Jim was absolutely furious when he spotted all our wedding presents in the shop window on his way home from work. I couldn't imagine why anybody would be so angry but I had to ask him to go to the shop to collect the furniture I'd swapped for the presents. Jim said, 'What say those relations come to visit?' And I replied, 'They're never going to come. Never in a hundred years are they ever going to come to Westport, and who cares if I don't have their chrome bloody whatsit?'

All those things whittle away at you. A few years later, when we shifted to Alexandra, I had to go ahead with the kids and he finished the last of the shift. I kept saying, 'Make sure that cane suite comes, make sure that cane suite comes.' And he left it behind. I don't think I've ever forgiven him for that.

One night in Westport I nearly burnt the house down. I took the ashes out of the coal range and it was pouring with rain so I left them in a cardboard box in the laundry. One of the miners going to work early the next morning banged on the door, yelling, 'Your house is on fire!' I asked, 'Is it very bad?' and he said, 'Yes! It's blazing!' We didn't have a phone so he rang the fire

engine for me from the house next door. But when it wasn't on fire my house was exceptionally clean and my brass was shining.

When we shifted to another house in Westport there was an English couple over the road who fought all the time. He was a miner and she would have to go down to the pub on her bike to get his pay packet before he drank it away. Their house was dirty and their kids all had fine, wispy hair and dirty faces. She had a broad northern English accent and she would call out as she got on her bike, 'I'm just away down, love. Would you keep your eye on the kids?' And the poor wee kids were locked in, standing at the window, looking out.

One night there were all these ructions coming from the house. There were always ructions, but this time it was particularly bad and I went over later to see if she was all right. He'd wrecked the whole house because she didn't have any food. She hadn't got his pay from him that week and he'd boozed it, so when he came home for his meal she said, 'We're going to have a square meal, here's half of it for you,' and she put an Oxo cube on his plate and cut it in half. I'd never known anything like that in my life. I was only just hanging in there myself and there was this drama I couldn't deal with over the road. She used to dump the dirty little kids on me; I'd feed them and wash their faces and hands, and try to tidy their hair. But then I'd throw the comb away. It was all just too much for me. It sounds pathetic but I just couldn't cope with somebody else's misery, knowing there was nothing I could do to help. That family seemed so alien, they may as well have come from the moon.

I was still going to estate auctions but I couldn't afford to buy much. I met a lovely lady and after we'd talked at a few auctions she asked me to go and visit her, but I never actually went. I thought it was odd that someone like her, a bank manager's wife who dressed so differently to me, who had a good income and a lovely house and friends and people for dinner, would want me to come to her house. She visited me once and I polished everything before she arrived. We had a lovely old wooden house but I had very little in it and the coal range smutted that day. She was wearing a beautiful white velour hat and I was mortified because it was sprinkled with little black smuts from the range. I didn't see her for quite some time and then I bumped into her one day and said, 'Oh, you haven't been to the auctions for a while.' She told me her husband had died.

Then she said that she'd realised she didn't have any real friends but she had thought I was her friend. I didn't know that our conversations at the auctions had meant that much to her and I felt bad that I'd let her down. So that was another thing for me to learn . . . don't make assumptions about people based on what they have or don't have.

There were some quiet pleasures to be had in Westport. I really enjoyed cooking on my coal range. I baked and I had a big vegetable garden and kept hens. During my wanderings I'd met people who had hens and I talked to them about it, and got some fertile eggs and sat them under bantams. I lost quite a few because of electrical storms — the thunder and lightning destroys the chickens in the eggs. I had other failures because I kept the broody hens in a lovely little warm straw-filled box in the concrete garden shed, on the concrete floor. Dad explained to me that not enough moisture got through so the eggshells were too hard and dry for the little chickens to get out. By learning from these basic mistakes I started a lifelong hobby of keeping backyard poultry.

We sometimes fished off the wharf and went whitebaiting in the Buller River, but my life revolved around going to the library, going to Plunket with the children, shopping at the butcher around the corner, going to the deceased-estate auctions and buying the blue *English Woman's Weekly* for the serial and the clothing patterns.

I did my best in Westport but I missed my family dreadfully and felt that I was without support, direction and purpose. Having babies was a big enough fright but being married to someone who wouldn't discuss anything with me, let alone whether or not we would have any more children, just made it worse. Now I know a number of other women who have been in that position, but at the time I felt incredibly alone.

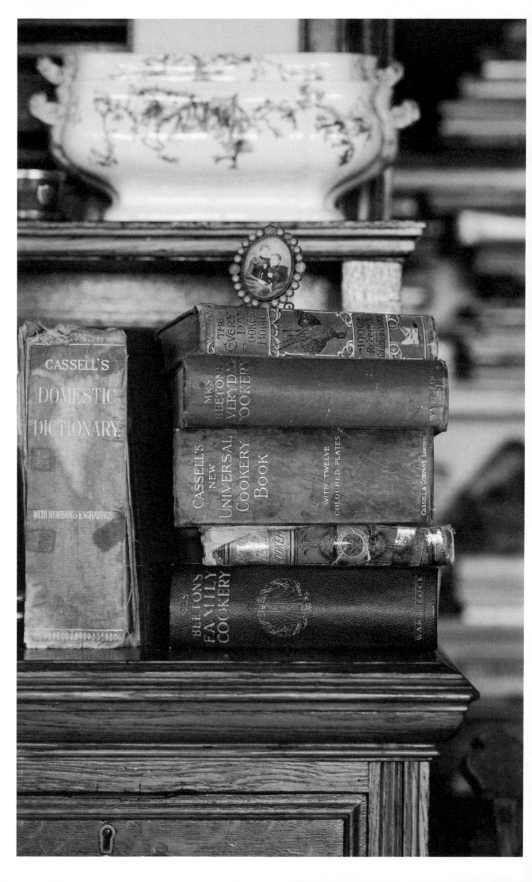

MY MOTHER
SENT US ADS FOR
JOBS SHE THOUGHT
WOULD BRING US
CLOSER TO HOME.
ONE WAS FOR
A REFRIGERATION
ENGINEER IN
ALEXANDRA, ABOUT
200 KILOMETRES
FROM OAMARU IN
THE DRY HEART OF
CENTRAL OTAGO.

3

THE GYPSY OF CENTRAL

There was an air link between the two towns, so in 1965 we shifted again. I never warmed to Alexandra. There was hardly anything old there; it was a town of neat gardens and shiny windows, a tidy place with bland modern houses. I didn't ever feel at home.

Besides, I had a wardrobe of jandals and raincoats from the Coast and there weren't too many others who looked like me. We rented a very old, very small biscuit-tin of a house with embossed zinc panels on the ceilings and walls. It was as cold as charity when we arrived in winter along with the hoar frosts (Alexandra's winter temperatures range from -6°C to 15°C and soar to 35°C in the summer). The water pipes were frozen for most of the day; they thawed by about three o'clock and started to freeze again by four, so washing babies' napkins took a huge effort. I would hang everything on the clothesline if the sun was shining or in the garage; either way it would freeze solid. When I picked Jim's overalls off the line they'd snap in half. It was shocking.

The coming of spring in Central Otago was one of the most beautiful things I'd ever seen. I used to take the kids into the hills around Alexandra; we found abandoned miner's cottages squatting among the wild thyme and briar roses, and at that time of the year the old spring gardens were starting to bloom. There were snowdrops and japonica, and quince, apple, cherry, plum and pear trees galore. I would just sit there and daydream about how it must have been when the goldminers first arrived in the 1860s.

ABOVE

My children. From left:
Martin, Brendon and Kirston.
A travelling photographer
took this photo and removed
Martin's freckles.

LEFT

Martin with his freckles.

BELOW

Martin and Kirston on
the Manorburn Dam,
Alexandra.

ABOVE LEFT

With the three kids
in Duntroon. Cousin
Llewellan Raitt peeping
around the door.

LEFT

From left:
Martin, Kirston and
their cousin Joanne Ross
at the biscuit-tin house.

BELOW

Dunstan House in 1968.
Jaycee exchange visitors on
each end, with me, Brendon,
Kirston and Martin.

I'd walk the kids up the Cromwell Gorge on the far side of the Clutha River long before there was talk about damming it and we'd camp in the little huts. The first time we went there we'd brought sausages and sandwiches with us but I'd put the basket on the roof of the car when we'd stopped to get fruit. As I drove up Fruitgrowers Road to where we were going to start our walk, the basket must have fallen off. I decided we'd have to forage for our food; we found freshwater lobsters, eels and watercress in the Clutha and cooked them in the frying pan.

I was happy exploring the high, dry hills around Alexandra but it was an aimless life. I didn't know I had other choices so, like thousands of young New Zealand mothers in the 1960s, I threw myself into learning all sorts of traditional domestic skills like carding and spinning wool, knitting and sewing. I loved learning to make beautiful things from raw materials but it was also something I had to do because my children were really feeling the cold in Central after the warm, wet weather on the Coast.

Cooking was also something I loved doing and wanted to get better at. The butcher and grocer became my friends in Alexandra, just as they had in Westport. Jock Braidwood was a really great butcher. The first time I went into his shop I was amazed to find that he made his own salamis and worsts. He told me that he'd discovered salami a few years before, in the early 1960s, when he was on holiday in Ingham, a little town in northern Queensland. Most people in the town were Italians who had arrived to work in the sugar-cane fields. Jock said he went into a shop and smelt something absolutely delicious — the rich garlic scent of salamis piled on countertops and even hanging from the ceiling. He said he'd never seen or smelt anything like it. He started talking to the owner, who gave him a few of her recipes because he said he'd like to see if he could introduce them into Central Otago.

When he got back to Alex, Jock made his salami from pork bellies with plenty of fat and meat that he'd pickled with buckets of garlic. After a while a lot of Dutch people started coming into the shop; they taught him how to make worsts, which became another line for him. His Dutch customers spread the word and soon he had people coming from as far away as Dunedin and Invercargill to buy his salami and worsts, but he said the restaurants

334   THE DICTIONARY OF COOKERY.

SUPPER, BILL OF FARE FOR A BALL, FOR 60 PERSONS
(for Winter).

Left side (top to bottom): Lobster Salad. — Two Roast Fowls, cut up. — Lobster Salad. — Two Roast Fowls, cut up. — Lobster Salad.

Right side (top to bottom): Lobster Salad. — Two Roast Fowls, cut up. — Lobster Salad. — Two Roast Fowls, cut up. — Lobster Salad.

Left	Centre	Right
	BOAR'S HEAD, garnished with Aspic Jelly.	
Fruited Jelly.	Mayonnaise of Fowl.	Charlotte Russe.
Small Pastry.	Small Ham, garnished.	Biscuits.
	Iced Savoy Cake.	
Vanilla Cream.	Epergne, with Fruit.	Fruited Jelly.
Prawns.	Two Boiled Fowls, with Béchamel Sauce.	Prawns.
Biscuits.	Tongue, ornamented.	Small Pastry.
Custards, in glasses.	Trifle, ornamented.	Custards, in glasses.
	Raised Chicken Pie.	
	Tipsy Cake.	
Fruited Jelly.	Roast Pheasant.	Swiss Cream.
Meringues.	Epergne, with Fruit.	Meringues.
Raspberry Cream.	Galantine of Veal.	Fruited Jelly.
Small Pastry.	Tipsy Cake.	Biscuits.
	Raised Game Pie.	
Custards, in glasses.	Trifle, ornamented.	Custards, in glasses.
	Tongue, ornamented.	
Prawns	Two Boiled Fowls, with Béchamel Sauce.	Prawns.
Biscuits.		Small Pastry.
	EPERGNE, WITH FRUIT.	
Fruited Jelly.	Iced Savoy Cake.	Blancmange.
	Small Ham, garnished.	
	Mayonnaise of Fowl.	
Charlotte Russe.	Larded Capon.	Fruited Jelly.

Note.—When soup is served from the buffet, Mock Turtle and Julienne may be selected. Besides the articles enumerated above, Ices, Wafers, Biscuits, Tea, Coffee, Wines, and Liqueurs will be required. Punch à la Romaine may also be added to the list of beverages.

ABOVE & RIGHT

Pages from *Beeton's All About Cookery Illustrated*.

and pubs in Queenstown and Wanaka were slow to pick up on any of the new products. In later years I made sure they were always on the table at Dunstan House and Olivers.

Jock and his wife dine at the Moeraki restaurant from time to time and he likes to remind me that back in the mid-1960s, before I'd got into the restaurant business, I was known as the Gypsy of Central because I wore long colourful skirts with velvet waistcoats and had a crop of fuzzy blonde hair.

Although I added salami and worst to the family diet, I mostly

Almonds and Raisins.

Raspberries and Strawberries.

Filberts and Cobs.

Gooseberries.

Peaches and Apricots.

Apples and Pears.

Walnuts and Brazil Nuts.

Figs and Dates.

Plums and Greengages.

Oranges.

Mulberries.

Blackberries.

Currants.

Epergne.

Cherries.

cooked traditional pioneer dishes at home because I'd discovered beautiful old colonial cookery and domestic economy books. One of my early favourites was *Cassell's Household Guide*, which was published in the 1860s. It lays out the management of servants and kitchens and is full of wonderful old recipes. I learnt to make things like oxtail stews and colonial goose, and I nearly perfected my soups.

I was lucky to meet Mrs Glad McArthur, an Alexandra identity who wrote gardening and cooking columns for the *Central Otago News*. Mrs McArthur's grandparents, Richard and Ellen Dawson, had settled at Conroy's Gully near Alexandra in the 1860s and introduced the Dawson cherry to the region, a cherry so sweet and juicy with a rich burgundy colour that it was and still is the pride of Otago cherries. With her wonderful knowledge of pioneer cooking, Glad McArthur became my new Mrs O'Dea.

When I first met her I told her about my soup-making, and she said I didn't have to grate my thumbs and knuckles off when I was preparing the vegetables. She suggested I just cut them into chunks and use a potato masher after cooking. Learning that trick saved so much time and it made soup-making much more fun. Mrs McArthur also helped me to develop a good working knowledge of the herbs of the region. I already had some idea of their possibilities from my family and Mrs O'Dea but Mrs McArthur gave me the names of books to get from the library. I read everything I could find about their culinary and medicinal uses. I'd walk for hours on the hills gathering wild thyme, teasels and woolly mullein and would win first prize for my herb collections at the Alexandra flower shows. There was a little mud-block shed at the side of our biscuit-tin house where I hung the herbs and wild flowers to dry. I thought I might earn some money by setting up a mail-order business selling armfuls of these beautiful wild weeds but the first place I approached wanted them sprayed red and green so they stayed safe in my shed.

The hot, dry summer climate in Alexandra is wonderful for pip and stone fruits, berries, currants and wild herbs. I used the recipes from my old cookbooks and made jams, sauces and thyme jellies for Christmas presents and school fairs, sealing the bottles with melted paraffin and making flour and water paste to stick the brown-paper labels to the jars.

It was while I was in Alex that I first thought about taking
a stand on environmental and heritage issues. The Alexandra
Jaycees were proposing to put an illuminated clock on a hill
above the town; it was to be 11 metres in diameter and visible from
8 kilometres away at night. They wanted Alexandra's slogan to be
'The Big Time Town' and their proposal had a lot of supporters as
well as a good number of vocal opponents. Letters of protest from
the artist Elizabeth Stevens were printed regularly in the *Central
Otago News* and as I read them I decided I wanted to meet her.
I loved the sense of space and *timelessness* I found in the hills; why
would we want something so artificial glaring down on the town?
But Jim was a Jaycee so when I said I wasn't in favour of the clock
he forbade me from getting involved in the protest. The realisation
that he believed he had the right to tell me what to think and how
to behave in public was another straw that would eventually break
the back of the marriage.

I visited Elizabeth to tell her I supported her position but that
I couldn't make my views known publicly. The clock was installed
on the hill in 1968 and Elizabeth and I became lifelong friends.
When I shifted to Moeraki in 1999 she sent me two beautiful
watercolour landscapes of the Moeraki harbour that she had
painted about 40 years earlier. I had them framed and hung them
on the wall in the restaurant. I was very sad when, not too long
after that, she developed Alzheimers; she has since passed away.

Meanwhile I was still collecting beautiful old bits and pieces,
fossicking in second-hand shops looking for preserving jars and
bottles and anything else that appealed to me. One day when I
went to buy fruit from an old mud-brick packing shed I looked
up at the rafters and saw an oval pedestal table with four claw
feet. I couldn't believe it! The fruit sellers had put it up there
years ago and had long since forgotten about it. They said it had
belonged to their mother, and when they got it down for me and
I saw the cedar base and kauri top I asked if I could buy it. Poor
Jim! I didn't have anything other than the grocery money and
I spent that on the table. Such things don't make for a good
relationship. But I've still got the table and it's made me happy
for a long time.

By this time I had a little car of my own, a Citroën that I bought
in Ranfurly for £25. Getting a car was a big deal for me, but it had
been in a shed for years and it looked like it. I half-sanded it down
but didn't have the money to get it painted so people would look at
it and raise their eyebrows. I'd think to myself, Oh well, at least it's
paid for! I loved it; the kids could be picked up from the sandpit,
put in the back of the car and away we would go!

❖

Not long after I bought the car I discovered Clyde. It's only
7 kilometres up the road from Alexandra but I'd never been there.
Wow! Clyde, what a discovery: its main street lined with beautiful old schist buildings, hotels, cottages, stone walls.

The township had taken root when thousands of goldminers
poured into the area after a big strike in the Clutha River in 1862.
There were very few trees, so they built their shops, pubs and
houses first in calico fabric and later with the flat, lichen-covered
stone that lay all over the countryside.

I wandered along the main street, soaking up the details in
the near derelict Tinker's Cottage, Dr Morice's home, the Masonic
Lodge, the Hartley Arms Hotel, Naylor's General Store, the
Commercial Hotel and the Dunstan Hotel. I was laughing and
crying at the same time. This was such a beautiful display of
New Zealand's colonial history all lined up in one narrow street
but it was like a ghost town.

I'd gone to Clyde because I'd seen an advertisement asking for
people to pick wild thyme for the Briar Herb Factory in the town.
Kirston was going to school but I still had the two little boys at
home; Jim said I could do it as long as I picked in a safe fenced
paddock so I wouldn't lose them. I never told him that I just went
where the wild thyme was, all over the hills. I sold the thyme to
Mr Brown at the factory where he threshed it using beautiful old
wooden machinery painted with folk-art designs.

I can't remember how much I was paid but because I was working
outside I got lovely and brown while I was doing it and besides, the

thyme smelt wonderful. After I took the bundles back to the herb factory I'd browse around the town, discovering more and more every day. Then I'd have to get back, pick up Kirston and cook the tea but I couldn't wait to get started again the next day. Jim would say to me, 'By the time you've paid for your petrol you won't make any money.' All those deadly boring things.

I couldn't believe it when I discovered that Ben Naylor's house and the general store that fronted onto Sunderland Street were for sale. The whole property was surrounded by a tall stone wall, a dense hedge and huge walnut trees so I didn't realise that it covered about half a hectare — nearly a whole town block including eight stone buildings. The price was £6000 and I asked Dad if he could lend me some money to buy it. But parents don't want you to do hard things; after he looked at all the tin roofs and the general state of the place he wasn't encouraging. He said he'd buy a section for me on Bridge Hill in Alexandra and I could build a comfortable modern house but that's not what I wanted to do.

Ron Jackson, the local vet, and his wife, June, bought the property instead. I'd met June at playcentre, and I asked her if they would consider letting me buy the barn. She was very nice and explained that they had plans for the barn but suggested that I look at 'the Dunstan', the hotel over the road, to see if I was interested in buying that.

A few days later, after I'd delivered the thyme to Mr Brown, I noticed that the door to the hotel was a wee bit open. I went inside and called out, and the owners, two lovely elderly people, agreed to show me around.

The Dunstan Hotel was built in 1900 to replace the original building that had been on the section since 1863. The new hotel was a two-storey schist building with a wooden wrap-around veranda and a beautiful Georgian staircase with 10 little bedrooms leading off the landing at the top. There was a bathroom upstairs but the water cylinder in the roof had rusted and fallen right through the ceiling, down through the floor and into the little bar downstairs, just above the cellar. The old billiards room downstairs had been turned into a flat with a bathroom and there were a couple of people boarding there. The owners told me the billiards room had once been the 'travellers' room' because commercial travellers would set their wares out for people to buy. The kitchen, next to the dining room, was a wooden lean-to with a double-oven coal range and a rotten floor, while the scullery was outside in another lean-to.

But it was all just so good! I asked the owners if they might like to sell, and after negotiating over a few days they said they would, for the sum of £4000. I'd learned a little bit by then so I asked if they'd consider leaving something in as a second mortgage, and then I'd borrow the rest of the money. They agreed and Mum and Dad cashed in a £400 insurance policy they'd been paying for me. Then I went to the bank, borrowed the rest of the money and bought it.

I was a bad enough wife beforehand but after I bought the hotel I became impossible. Surprisingly, Jim handled it quite well at first because I sold him on the idea that we could turn it into a business. It had no plumbing and no kitchen but it did have boarders so, as far as I was concerned, I had a bed and breakfast. We shifted in during the winter of 1967, just as decimal currency was being introduced.

I really wanted to hold onto the original name, the Dunstan Hotel, but someone else had laid claim to that for another property so I called it Dunstan House. We had very little furniture so as soon as I got any money I'd visit some of the local farms I'd driven past and say, 'I've seen those iron beds under the hedges; would you sell them to me?' They'd reply, 'Oh yeah, they went out there years ago . . . yes, of course you can have them.' And then they'd say, 'We used to have more but they've been used in the concrete drive for reinforcing', or 'We chucked all of them down the gully.'

There wasn't any money to rebuild the wrecked kitchen so I took over the room upstairs where the former owners had kept the coal range with a water tank at the side. I eventually bought a second-hand electric range but I cooked nearly all the meals on that coal range for seven years. Next to the kitchen I put a breakfast room and filled it with lovely old wooden tables and chairs. A gingham frill along the front of the mantelpiece over the coal range and old ashets propped against the wall on top were the finishing touches. It was just beautiful.

LEFT
From left:
Me, Kirston, Martin
and Brendon.

BELOW LEFT
The Pleace brothers,
who replaced the chimneys
and removed the old kitchen
at Dunstan House.

BELOW RIGHT
The back of Dunstan House,
with the boarders' annexe at
left and the old wooden
kitchen in centre.

BOTTOM
Martin and Brendon on the
building site — no shoes!

Transforming
Dunstan House

Dunstan House after the
kitchen was removed.

Michael and Kevin Sullivan,
my 'Sullivan Kids' cousins, in
the wreckage of the kitchen.

The front of Dunstan House
on the main street of Clyde.
I showed the boys
squashed rabbits on the
road and told them that's
what they'd end up like
if they fell off the verandah!
It worked.

I collected old bits of furniture from estate auctions in Alexandra: iron beds, hanging lamps, lovely old linens and vintage curtains. Slowly it came together. I was having the best time.

The guests always appreciated the food at Dunstan House. At first I perfected the breakfasts for the boarders and overnight guests. Eventually I had eight boarders living in what had been the old stables at the back of the house and we had good fun together. I made their lunches and every now and then I'd play tricks like putting small squares of newspaper in one of their sandwiches or deliberately forgetting to cook the supposedly hard-boiled eggs.

After a while I started offering dinners as well as bed and breakfast. My cooking knowledge had come from my family, the Mrs O'Deas, the Mrs McArthurs and my growing collection of wonderful old nineteenth-century domestic economy books with their recipes for wholesome, filling dishes. I followed my instinct that the food had to come from Central Otago: wild rabbit with thyme, game birds, veal and ham pies, steak and kidney puddings, and traditional desserts like custards and fruit puddings, tarts and pies. I sourced all my fruit and vegetables from local people and had a small garden with lots of parsley and herbs for soup. Twenty years later, when the slow-food movement arrived, I was able to put a label on the way I'd been cooking for years.

Meanwhile, I was just about bursting with excitement about Clyde and its history. The wild, dry countryside with its towering hills covered in thyme, briar rose, rosehips, rabbits, mushrooms, opium and Californian poppies, mint, and rowan and elderberries, the hot blue skies in summer and the winter snow and hoar frosts made me feel so alive. I wanted to know more about the streets of old stone buildings. Who had lived in them a hundred years ago? What was life like in Clyde in the 1860s? There was so much history attached to the town, so many stories on the tombstones in the cemeteries and so many people were still alive who could tell me stories.

Soon after we arrived I read *Early Days in Central Otago* by Robert Gilkison, the first lawyer in the goldfields. That's when I really came to understand exactly what I had in Dunstan House and Clyde. The hotel had originally been a weatherboard and

calico hotel known as The Dunstan with a dining room, drawing room and smoking room as well as a theatre where, people say, a brass band and dancing girls performed on a Saturday night. It was also the booking office, stables and accommodation for the Cobb & Co passengers travelling by horse-drawn coach on the three-day journeys between Dunedin, Arrowtown and Queenstown.

The new Dunstan Hotel was built on the original site in 1900 and it was the first of its kind in Central Otago. The stonemason, Thomas Wilkinson, used schist quarried from the gorge end of Clyde. Albert Fountain, the staircase builder and joiner, sourced native hardwood timber from the Upper Wanaka region for the beautiful central staircase. I met an old man in Clyde, Charles Atfield senior, who said he'd ridden his horse up the stairs and around the interior balcony in the wild old days. The Dunstan Hotel was the social centre of Clyde for thousands of miners and townspeople for decades. The hotel was closed in 1937 and the building had hardly been used until I bought it 30 years later.

Once I'd settled in Clyde, I would talk to people about the town's history. I'd say, 'Just look at this place! Look how beautiful it is. We need to get together and work out how to maintain these buildings — find buyers who'll look after them and set up businesses.' They just couldn't see that the old part of town had any value. One guy said, 'I've done my best here, I've tried to modernise the place.'

I remember Bill senior and Mel Annan, the publicans, pulling down the old drystone wall so customers could park cars on the front lawn. At the time the Manapouri lines were being built, with pylons marching over our beautiful hills, and down in the village our old buildings were being demolished to build car parks. And after June and Ron bought the pub they were going to buy and demolish my Dunstan Hotel and use the vacant lot for a car park. Yet of course they were not bad people; that was just how people thought in 1967. We became very good friends over the years.

Another old friend, Arty Guy, was descended from a family who worked as interpreters for the Chinese goldminers. He and his wife lived in a beautiful little stone cottage and he'd say, 'I don't care, girl. If I win the Golden Kiwi I'll get some good

racehorses. And then I'll push this house over and build my wife a decent one. She's had nine kids in this house.'

Within a few months I'd set up the Clyde Promotion Group. I showed all the historic sites to the two local motel owners but they were only mildly interested. Most people couldn't understand why I was so worked up about them. I went to the Prime Minister and told him what I wanted him to do for Clyde. He listened politely but nothing happened, so in 1969 I started visiting Bert Walker, the Minister of Tourism, to talk about what was being pulled down. I became a councillor on the Vincent County Council, the forerunner of the Central Otago District Council. Clyde was perfect; everything was still there, untouched by progress. I was just trying to make sure people understood what they had and why they shouldn't bulldoze it. As far as I'm concerned, there's no sound more blood-chilling than a bulldozer ripping through old stone buildings.

Within three years of opening Dunstan House I was working alongside Dr Neil Begg from the Historic Places Trust, trying to have the old buildings in Clyde placed on its register of protected places. I began bombarding Bert Walker with letters saying, 'You're building Shantytown on the West Coast for, I don't know, $29,000 or something, and if you give me $5000 I'll save a whole town.' I went to Wellington to see him three times. The first time I saw him he was getting ready for an overseas trip and his offsider was putting candles in the shape of the heads of Maori chiefs in his suitcase! I thought, This isn't the man for me to be talking to. Another time I was in a taxi in Christchurch and I said to the driver, 'Where does the Minister of Tourism live?' We went to his house and there was one of those big wooden butterflies on the wall and a seal with a silver ball on its nose in the garden. These days having a butterfly on your wall and a seal with a ball on its nose in your garden might be very dashing and the height of kitsch but then, when they were for real, it wasn't such a good look. Especially for the Minister of Tourism.

I was involved in just about anything that celebrated the history of the town and its surroundings. The fabulous stone fruit and soft fruit industries were part of that heritage so I made elderflower and elderberry wine and joined an amateur winemakers' club. I was convinced that the club should be named after Jean Desire Feraud, who in 1864 set up the first winery in Central Otago on his property, Monte Christo Gardens, opposite what is now the Clyde cemetery. When they called it the Central Otago Winemakers' Club, I lost interest. It seemed obvious to me that we should be celebrating the history of the area and although we did take a tour of the remains of Monte Christo to see where Feraud's grapevines had been, the club wasn't convinced. The others happily went on making fruit wine and I remained friends with them, but the attraction for me was to the colourful Jean Desire Feraud. By now I was so busy that I didn't have much time to socialise anyway.

Because Ron and June Jackson lived just over the road, we used to look after each other's kids. If June couldn't get home from the vet surgery, her children would come to my house. If any of my kids hurt themselves I'd send them to Ron to see if they needed to go to the doctor. He'd usually say something like, 'Oh, he looks all right to

me. I wouldn't worry about it.' Later, when I worked in Queenstown,
I sent Brendon to the doctor with Kirston and the doctor said to
him, 'Have you never been to a doctor before?' Brendon replied,
'No, Mum usually sends us to the vet.' Kirston was mortified.

After a year or two I opened an art gallery, exhibiting mostly
local painters, and also an antiques shop in Dunstan House.
Evan Blair had an excellent antiques shop in Oamaru and I sold on
commission for him as well as buying and selling on my own behalf.

From the beginning, just opening the doors and having kids
running in and out attracted a lot of attention. People would knock
on the door to ask if they could stay because at the time there was
very little accommodation in Alexandra and Clyde. In the seven
years I had Dunstan House I had guests from all over New Zealand
and around the world. The mountaineers Graham Dingle and
Murray Jones stayed in the early days; Murray taught my kids
to abseil off the veranda. His brother, Alan Jones, was one of my
boarders; he later tragically died in a mountaineering accident.

Bruno Lawrence and the band Blerta stayed too. I remember the
owners of the H&J Smith department store in Invercargill arriving in
their Range Rovers with their lovely dogs to make up hunting parties.
They bought me quail, chukka, pheasants, partridge, wild ducks
and guinea fowl and, even better, taught me how to prepare them.

The Australian Leader of the Opposition was brought to see
Dunstan House as an example of a successful New Zealand
tourism venture. The New Zealand official who arrived
beforehand brought a roll of red carpet and spread it out in front
of the hotel. Then he gave me a quick lesson in how to curtsey so
that I'd be prepared when this bloke got out of his big black car.
It was ridiculous to think that I had to curtsey to anyone in front
of half of the population of Clyde but I did it, very quickly
and very reluctantly.

About halfway through those seven years at Dunstan House
Jim and I began to live separately. He was off doing bigger and
better things with his refrigeration work; he had a workshop in
Clyde for a while but then he went to Invercargill and started a
refrigeration business in partnership with another guy making big
walk-in units. He came home less and less often and when he did
it was a nuisance. He'd bring a crowd for the weekend and they'd

Moeraki camping holiday, 1966. Check out the haircuts. When
you took your boys to the barber and gave instructions such as
— 'a young Prince Charles, like this please' — they nodded and
out the boys came with short back and sides.

Home for Christmas and winner of the
Mrs Friendly Bay pageant, Oamaru, 1967.
On my right is the judge, who was Miss
New Zealand at the time.

all have a jolly good time at the pub and I'd be left to clean up the mess. It's very hard to maintain a marriage when one person makes all the major decisions and forgets to consult the other person.

At this point I was financially independent of Jim. He never contributed to what I was doing; in fact, I contributed to his business. I decided I really needed a proper kitchen so we borrowed some money, which went into Jim's account, and he took it to buy a tin-bender for his refrigeration business that cost something like $7000 — quite a lot of money in those days. After that things were really not good between us.

I felt that if I didn't have a commercial kitchen I couldn't improve the business any further; I couldn't charge any more for my bedrooms because the facilities weren't good enough. The wiring was such that in order to cook the breakfast in the morning I had to turn off the bedroom heaters via the master switch in the kitchen. I did that for seven years while I tried to figure out how I could get a low-interest loan to pay for the upgrade.

The James Cook Hotel in Wellington was being built at the time for $20,000 a bedroom and I knew all I needed was $5000 to make my place perfect. It used to make me furious that the general interest rate for borrowing money was 9 per cent while big tourism ventures were paying only 4 per cent. It seemed obvious to me that businesses on Clyde's main street should qualify for the lower rate, so the buildings could be preserved intact and the town promoted as a tourism destination. I had files full of letters to anyone in government I thought might listen to my views on regional tourism.

By 1974 I felt I could go no further. I just gave up on the world of finance and Dunstan House, wanting our 'real' New Zealand recognised and protected. I was 34 years old. The people who bought it owned a house in Invercargill and part of the deal was that we had to buy their property. I left everything in place in Dunstan House, all the collected treasures: hanging lamps, iron beds, slate billiard table. It was in fact a colonial Olveston. It nearly broke my heart but I decided that because children are meant to have a father I would go to Invercargill to be with Jim. So we headed off on a new adventure, and I promised the kids we would finally be able to go on holidays and their school camps together. I made a bonfire of all my correspondence to the various MPs and off we went to Invercargill.

THROUGHOUT
THE 18 MONTHS
I SPENT IN
INVERCARGILL
DURING 1974–75,
JIM SULLIVAN
WAS DETERMINED
TO PUNISH ME
FOR THE
INDEPENDENCE
I'D HAD IN CLYDE.

4

A WHOLE NEW WORLD OF FOOD

Jim and I hadn't had much of a relationship for the past seven years and now he was obsessed by the fact that the bank manager had persuaded me to put some of the money from the sale of Dunstan House into my personal account. It sent him into a frenzy because he had no access to it.

Jim had spent most of what we'd made from the sale of Dunstan House on his refrigeration business and clearing a lot of debts I hadn't known about. One day he arrived home with a huge left-hand-drive two-door Chevrolet and the car salesman, who was holding the ownership papers. The two of them stood over me until I added my signature to the cheque and the salesman said, 'I'm sure he'll let you drive it.' In fact I did drive it — twice — plus I got to keep the car salesman's biro I'd signed the cheque with. The car went 18 kilometres to the gallon and cost as much as the house to buy.

The first time I drove it was on a trip to Oamaru to see Mum and Dad. The car was so big I was able to pick up every hitchhiker on the road. It was an exciting trip. Try manoeuvering a left-hand-drive car with two little boys as co-pilots shouting, 'Yes! You can pass, Mum', and then pulling out into the oncoming traffic only to have them yell, 'You can do it, Mum! Boot it!' When I refilled at a service station one of the guys at the pump said, 'You married to an Arab?'

My dad said Jim had had a private bank in me while I was at Dunstan House and he was dopey not to look after me when we moved to Invercargill. Jim hadn't supported his family in any

Better times.

way while we were in Clyde and now he couldn't handle his role as the provider. He became nasty towards the children and he tormented me.

He constantly told me that I was a fraud and a failure in every aspect of my life. He would say, 'You can fool 99.9 per cent of the people but I know what you're really like. You can't fool me. I've got more power and potential in my little finger than you have in your whole body.'

After a while I came to believe that he was probably right. He insisted that I was a stupid, ugly know-it-all who couldn't make the money he gave me stretch to run a household, when in fact he would either refuse to give me any money, or hide it somewhere in the house for me to find.

He thought he was an honourable man because he never hit me. I would draw strength from a framed photograph of my dad on the mantelpiece. I'd say, 'You won't get away with this, Jim.' But he'd jeer at me, 'You try to prove it. You haven't got a mark on you.'

For some reason he wanted me to be the one to desert the marriage. He'd sometimes come in at all hours and then tell me to hurry up and decide when I was leaving because he couldn't bring anyone home while I was there. Sometimes he didn't come home at all. But I had three children, no money and nowhere to go, and I certainly didn't want my parents to know what a failure I was as a wife. He wanted me to go to a lawyer to end our marriage, and gave me a list of things I was meant to say. I went to the lawyer but I put my own position forward and in the end he was the one to leave.

Most of my treasures were still in storage in Clyde but I sold the ones I'd brought with me to raise enough money to feed the children and pay the bills. Jim would arrive at the door and say 'How are you paying for food? Where are you getting the money?' I'd say, 'I sold two old clocks,' and he'd start yelling that they weren't mine to sell.

On Christmas Eve he told our son Martin he was flying to Australia for a holiday and that he'd leave a cheque for us with the lawyer. It was after five o'clock when I heard this and we all raced down to the lawyer's office but they had closed for the three weeks over Christmas. Through the glass pane in the front door we could see an envelope with my name on it lying on the floor. Jim had slipped it under the door after everyone had gone home.

It was a very difficult time for the kids. As well as having to deal with the tension in their new home, they missed their friends in Clyde and hated the cold, wet weather in Southland.

There were still a few light moments. One afternoon they were playing in the backyard where we had a little fish pond, and they came running to me yelling, 'Mum, Mum, there's a duck in the fish pond.' As soon as I saw it I shouted, 'That's not a duck — that's our tea!' They were squealing and laughing as I tackled the duck. I chopped its head off, plucked it and stuffed it, and we ate a grand meal that night. In the morning I heard a description of our duck on the radio in the lost-and-found pets announcements; I quickly turned off the radio so the kids wouldn't find out.

Even after he left the house I was terribly afraid of Jim, of what he might do to me or the children. He was becoming increasingly aggressive and began threatening to go to court to claim custody of the kids. I was constantly anxious, and I came close to developing bulimia without knowing there was a word for it. I'd eat so that the children wouldn't think there was anything wrong and then I'd vomit. I remember taking the kids to the movies and seeing myself in a long mirror. I couldn't believe that it was me; my legs were like broom handles with saucers for knees.

Jim's constant threats that he would take the children or get them (whoever *they* were) and take them from me finally got to me. I began to think that he was right, that I was deluded or just plain incompetent. I was falling to pieces.

One day I found myself sitting with my kids in the laundry after I'd masked up the windows, preparing myself to turn on the gas. I thought the only way out was to end it for all of us. I knew he didn't love his kids and it seemed I was incapable of looking after them. But I couldn't go through with it.

I rang Lifeline and they arranged for me to see a minister. He was kind and understanding but when he said, 'Well, we'll kneel and pray,' I replied, 'God is not going to get me out of this mess but I promise you if I get out of this mess, I will thank God. I'm not going to come here to pray to God. I would go to my parents but because my father loves me, he won't be tough on me. I need a stranger; I need to be told honestly where I'm at and what I've done wrong.'

It took me years to recover from being married. Even today, no matter how confident I appear, there's always a voice in my mind saying that I'm fooling 99.9 per cent of the people.

I couldn't pay the bills so the power was disconnected and a man from the power board came to see me. He was also a member of the Society of St Vincent De Paul and said he made a point of calling on people in my situation to see if there was anything he could do to help. When I told him what was happening he arranged to have the power reconnected in my name and said I'd be eligible for the Domestic Purposes Benefit, which had just been introduced by the government to help solo mothers. I'd never heard of it! This lovely man made an appointment for me at the Department of Social Welfare.

I was incredibly grateful to receive the benefit, but I soon realised I couldn't raise three kids on $45.95 a week. I began looking for work to supplement what the government was giving me. I applied for jobs cleaning motels but the owners wouldn't take me on because I had three children. They'd say, 'You might be able to work after the kids go to school but what say the kids get sick? You won't be reliable.'

I applied for jobs at restaurants but they wanted a person to work over the tea hour and that's the time when I needed to be at home with the children. And the most you were allowed to earn was about $18 a week or it was taken off your benefit, which meant that you just couldn't get ahead.

The turning point came when my friend Maureen Smith, who lived in Queenstown and was raising six children on her own, told me to go and see Margaret and Keith Gerrard at the Railway Hotel. The Gerrards were the kindest, loveliest people I'd met in a long time. They gave me work cooking and waitressing, and slowly my self-esteem began to return.

Margaret served beautifully prepared and presented breakfasts and simple evening meals for a handful of guests so I didn't learn a lot about big hotel kitchens but she was absolutely organised — there was no wastage. Once Margaret and Keith got to know me they would go away for the weekend and I'd mind the place. They were happy for me to bring the children there on the weekends and we were all well fed. Often Margaret would give me a preserving jar of her beautiful soup and a loaf of bread to take home for the children's tea.

Margaret also had the most impeccable taste, which showed in everything she did. There were little silver toast racks on the breakfast tables, the toast was elegantly cut, the butter was served in little silver dishes; everything was just beautifully done.

It was all very genteel except for the little bit of business Mr Gerrard conducted on the side. The hotel was built in 1896 to cater for the many rail passengers of the time, and it was huge. The ground floor had been refurbished but the top level was as it had been for years; some of the sailors used to book rooms up there for two hours at a time. Keith endeavoured to conceal this from Margaret but he told me he was doing it to increase his turnover — he got the same price for two hours as for 24. It made me laugh because it was so much fun being back with real people.

The Gerrards didn't get involved in my problems but they knew what was happening. They were very dignified and they gave me courage.

The first time I had to go to court I bought myself a pair of green suede wedge-heeled shoes. I was very skinny and I was wearing a green body shirt and a green six-gored skirt, with a brown wooden bracelet, and Margaret Gerrard said to me, 'I think you look too well turned out to go asking for maintenance money to support the kids.' I said to her, 'The only things that cost money were the shoes; the rest of the clothes are remodelled op-shop bargains.' I didn't get changed.

My parents had come from Oamaru to support me because Jim was going for custody of the boys but had said I could keep Kirston if I could prove that I could behave myself, whatever that meant. When I got to the court I could see I wasn't meant to be there. I looked at people who were so dejected and I knew that I just needed some help to get up out of that hole I was in. Before we were called into court Jim's lawyer put a proposal to me — if I gave Jim two chairs and a desk that I had in the house, they would stop the custody wrangle. I refused. The judge said, 'Why won't you give him the two chairs?' I replied, 'There is only one of him and four of us, and we only have two chairs.' And the judge smiled.

Of course I was given custody of all the children plus $6 a week maintenance, but I knew I had to get out of Invercargill. There is a mechanism in most women that kicks in when their children are vulnerable. When Maureen said she had arranged a job for me in Queenstown I rented out the house, took my last $60 and packed the kids into the Chev. (I'd liberated it from Jim by simply not returning it after picking up the boys from school camp that day.) The car was now a wreck because Jim had used it as a work truck and had let his young employees hoon around in it. The tyres were marginal and it was making a troublesome noise that I couldn't identify.

As we drove out of town the kids were acting up because they were leaving new friends without saying goodbye. They were still grizzling when we got to Lumsden, where the Chev broke down. I told them it was crunch time. We could fix the car with our $60 and go on to Queenstown or abandon the Chev where it was and take our $60 back to Invercargill. The Chev won. The mechanic's wife fed us while trying to cheer up three surly kids and we headed for Queenstown with a promise that, as soon as I could, I'd send the rest of the money for the repairs.

'56 Chevy, Clyde.

In the mid-1970s, Queenstown was still the place where people from Dunedin and Invercargill had their modest holiday homes. They came in summer for boating, fishing and swimming in the magnificent Lake Wakatipu and in winter to ski at Coronet Peak and the Remarkables, the aptly named mountain range that rises above the lake. The beauty of the area drew buses full of tourists and even some foreign film crews but in terms of the permanent population, it was still a small town. I think there might have been only one or two Four Square stores; the first real supermarkets didn't appear until the 1990s.

Our new home was a house on a poultry farm in Frankton, about 10 kilometres from Queenstown. I was working split shifts as a housemaid and kitchenhand at the Travelodge where Maureen worked as a housemaid and laundress. She always said her youngest son Craig was brought up there in a laundry basket. He's now a musician and wrote the massively popular kids' book *The Wonky Donkey*, and he and Maureen co-wrote *Willbee the Bumblebee*, his follow-up book.

After a while we moved into a little A-frame house in

Queenstown. I worked different shifts as a housemaid, waitress, kitchenhand and bartender at the Esplanade Hotel. With a lot of help from Kirston, who by then was nearly 14, I did keep the family fed and cared for despite working 'hospitality' hours.

I knew I had to get off the Domestic Purposes Benefit because I couldn't stand the bureaucratic wrangling. The $25 a week I received in rent from the Invercargill house was classed as income so I could earn only a little bit more without losing the benefit. However, I was renting a more expensive house in Queenstown so the Department of Social Welfare was giving me an accommodation benefit to cover my rent.

I went to the dole office and said, 'I don't want a supplementary benefit — I'll take care of my rent and balance it off against the $25 I get from the Invercargill house, but let me earn what I'm allowed without taking that $25 into account.' They couldn't make it work that way because of the paperwork. None of it made sense, so I thought, They can muck around with my money as much as they like, doing all this paperwork, taking some away and putting some back — I'm just going to earn whatever I can, whenever I can. No solo parent can live honestly on the DPB.

All my life I've been driven mad by wasting time complying with regulations that make no sense. I've had some very public set-tos with district councils and government departments over the years.

In this instance I decided to do things my own way so I got cash jobs as a contractor. I couldn't be bothered with trade union regulations either. I didn't want morning- and afternoon-tea breaks, double time on Sundays and extra money for doing split shifts. I was a contractor, I charged a minimum flat hourly rate and I worked all the hours available.

Fortunately the kids had developed a wild enthusiasm for skiing and were able to spend all weekend on Coronet Peak because of the generous ski passes available to local school-children. I went up with them the first few times and met the staff at the rental shop, who kept an eye on them and helped them get the right gear.

During the week I worked at the Esplanade and on Saturday and Sunday when the kids were skiing I worked at Number 8 Ballarat with David Williams.

David was the whiz-kid of the restaurant world in Queenstown in the mid-1970s. He was only 22 when he arrived on the scene after completing his hotel-management training with the Tourist Hotel Corporation (THC), working in some of the most prestigious hotels in the country. Since his time in Queenstown he's had any number of restaurants in Auckland and these days he and his wife have an Italian restaurant called Spago in Auckland's Britomart and another right next door to it called the General Store.

When David arrived in Queenstown, he and fellow chef Imre Toth set up the restaurant Upstairs and Downstairs in what was known as the Trading Post, the first shopping mall in town. It was situated in what had been the original picture theatre, which had an opening roof so audiences could enjoy the movies by starlight. The restaurant was located where the old screen would have been, a big open space at the end of the shopping arcade; people ate their meals 'upstairs and downstairs'. Imre, who was originally from Hungary, was a very well-known chef in Wellington and had worked at Orsinis before opening Plimmer House in the capital. The pair ran Upstairs and Downstairs together for about 18 months before David moved across the road and opened Number 8 Ballarat.

In the mid-1970s Queenstown had a permanent population of about 2000. The tourist season started on Boxing Day, with holidaymakers coming mainly from Invercargill and Dunedin and a few from Christchurch. The bus tours started mid-January and went through to the end of March. Then the restaurateurs and tourism operators, such as they were at the time, would wait it out until the end of June or the beginning of July when the first snow came, then they'd be busy until the spring thaw in mid-September. There were more bus tours through October and November, and then the businesses waited again until Boxing Day.

Queenstown had a number of restaurants in what was known as The Mall. Eichardt's Hotel, where most of the hospitality people gathered for pre-work drinks, was on the corner. There was the Continental restaurant, which served buffet food to hundreds of people in peak season, and on the left was the Golden Axe, which became Number 8 Ballarat. The Huntsman's Steakhouse came later. Marigold Miller was developing The

In front of
Number 8 Ballarat
with David
Williams and
friend Barbara
Coultan.

Packer's Arms out near Arrowtown and the Travelodge opened
opposite the Earnslaw Wharf. That was about the extent of the
restaurant scene.

At that time, the international hotels served a lot of classic
French and German cuisine such as tournedos Rossini (a French
steak dish) or chicken Kiev. Soups were still thickened with flour
and sauces were still done via emulsions or purées and those for
meats were velouté-based. Venison was still served with grilled
pears and cranberry jelly and there was very little variation from
the rule book. The usual menu consisted of things like shrimp
cocktail, scallops of veal with lemon wedges and paté with toast,
with the classic garnish of lemon and tomato wedges with a twist
of cucumber and a sprig of curly green parsley. There were a few
exceptions but for the most part those were your choices.

But the dishes that were served in restaurants before the new
wave opened were even more limited: porterhouse and fillet
steaks, chicken Maryland, a roast leg of lamb and that was about
it. There was little or no seafood to be had in Queenstown.

At Upstairs and Downstairs, David had introduced a menu that stayed in use for about five years. He served French onion and minestrone soups, a pepper steak (which he became well known for), a rump steak, chicken paprika and garlic scallops, which were famous. There would always be fresh vegetables on the menu but they were unbelievably hard to source. The menu included a green salad, his famous sautéed potatoes and a chocolate cake. At lunchtime people would queue for the steak sandwich and the open chicken sandwich. All this was considered revolutionary. Fresh, simple and delicious.

At Number 8 Ballarat, David introduced rack of lamb, served with a beautiful Provençal sauce. Then he sourced seafood from Invercargill and started doing seafood crêpes. He also introduced a lot of what he'd learned from the German and French chefs working for the THC.

I'd first met David when I was running Dunstan House. He came to stay because he'd heard about my little antique shop, and he said he was amazed by my decorative flair and attention to detail. We met again a few years later in Queenstown, in The Mall. David was the first person to put tables and chairs outside a restaurant, which was highly illegal and even made the national news, along with the fact that he charged 80 cents for a cup of percolated coffee — the most expensive in New Zealand at the time. I loved the idea of eating outside at little café tables so when David asked if I'd like to work at Number 8 Ballarat I jumped at the chance.

David was very discerning when he employed me as a waitress on the day shift because I was totally unsophisticated compared to the night-time waitresses. They all had little squeaky voices and tidy hairdos and teetered about on high heels, whereas I was more the country look. I ran the front of house and had a big influence on the look of the place, arranging the flowers and making sure everything was well presented in the restaurant.

The only wines available in Queenstown at the Eichardt's bottle store were Bakano, a McWilliams red; Cresta Doré, which was a McWilliams white; Blue Nun Liebfraumilch; Nedeburg; and a Moysten claret from Australia. It's hard to believe now but at the time there was no such thing as BYO and you couldn't get a licence, so nobody was allowed to drink in restaurants after six o'clock at night. Sergeant Maloney would wander around to make sure we were sticking to the regulations. David let people hide bottles under the tables but Sergeant Moloney found out so David's solution was to pour the wine into Temuka Pottery teapots and serve it in Temuka mugs.

While Imre and David were introducing me to another world of food and fun and fascinating people, Imre was also introducing New Zealand to garlic. When you talked to people, you always knew if they'd been to Upstairs and Downstairs because you could smell the garlic on their breath. And he cooked the most amazing steaks. He was interviewed on the TV news once because he wouldn't do a medium or well-done steak.

The owners of all the new restaurants in The Mall would walk along the street and look in the windows to see who was busy, and give a little wave if you caught their eye. I was beginning to understand the industry and it was fun. The way the restaurant kitchens were run was like nothing I'd ever seen, and Imre and David occasionally let me sit in the kitchen just to watch what they were doing. There was pan-cooking with the flames and the liqueurs, and the fast orders, the dockets and the tempers, the yelling and the pans being thrown, while out in the restaurants patrons were coming in at six o'clock, half-past six, half-past seven, eight o'clock and later for à la carte meals. We'd never seen steak knives and sizzle plates before. Imre hit the headlines again because he asked people to take their children and prams out of the restaurant.

One morning when I was doing the prep at Number 8 Ballarat before the chefs had arrived for the day, I realised we had no vinaigrette. The young lady working as a dishwasher was the daughter of the new owner of The Packer's Arms so I asked her to ring her dad to get a vinaigrette recipe. He wouldn't tell her because he said it was his competitive advantage.

I said, 'Well, ring him back and tell him that he doesn't have to tell me *their* recipe. I have no idea how to make vinaigrette. What's it made of? It can't be a secret!' Hard as it is to believe now, there were very few cookbooks around then so I didn't know where to get the information.

Service in restaurants back then was pretty basic too. At that time, both at Upstairs and Downstairs and Number 8 Ballarat, one person took the orders at the counter, called it and passed the docket to the kitchen, while the customer paid for it. The customer was given a cup of percolated coffee (espresso had yet to be introduced) and they were handed their cutlery. It seemed to be the best way to do it because we were so busy.

David and I worked well together, and he started to look for a new project we could get our teeth into. There was an early stone stable at the back of Number 8 Ballarat where it led into Cow Lane. David wanted to set up a pizza and spaghetti restaurant; there was no Italian food to be had in Queenstown at all back then. He decided to call it The Cow because of its location, and told the architect he wanted a space that looked like a cow shed crossed with a stable. The decision to use Queen Victoria's bust as the logo with the name inscribed below made the TV news as someone claimed it was bringing royalty into disrepute. You couldn't buy that kind of publicity!

I was involved in creating the look of the place and in developing the recipe for the pizza base, because I just couldn't find instructions anywhere. Surprisingly, even from day one, the result was a beautiful, thin, crisp pizza base. Pizza and spaghetti dishes were the height of trendy food in Queenstown at the time. David ran The Cow very successfully for six or seven years and it's still going to this day.

In those early days The Cow attracted all the glitterati who came to Queenstown — movie people, fashion designers, the golfer Arnold Palmer, the Saatchi brothers from London. Opening night, with all the big names in the film industry, was a lot of fun! There were a number of movies and TV commercials being made in the area so David bought a caravan through one of my contacts in Alexandra, had it converted into a mobile kitchen and began to do on-set catering for the movies being made around the lakes and in Central Otago.

Our weekend social life was hectic. After work at night everyone from the owners to the kitchen staff would move from one place to another to drink and wind down. We'd often go to the Skyline at the top of the gondola but everybody tried to end up at Frankton because it had a good bar and they brought in acts like the Howard Morrison Quartet. On summer nights I would accompany David and sit around the pool or in the house bar and I loved this new sophistication.

Meanwhile, during the week I was working at the Esplanade Hotel, which was managed by Harold and Joan Braine. Their son, John, came home to Queenstown after training as a chef in England and studying hotel management in Wellington. He was slender, quite good-looking and wore beautiful clothes. I didn't take much notice of him at first because he was 10 years younger than me and I'd never even thought of the possibility of our getting together.

A small group of us, including my friends Bill and Vaila Taylor and Maureen Smith, used to go up to the Skyline after work for a couple of hours at night if there was the promise of good music. One night Bill said to me, 'When are you going to give that young man a break? He absolutely adores you and you take no notice of him or you say to him, "We're going up there, come up later if you wish", and then you don't talk to him.'

I didn't mind that John was a colleague but the age difference really bothered me — by then I was 37 and he would have been 27. But he had some lovely qualities. Even though the kids never really got along with him, Kirston said to me once, 'It was good that John Braine came into our lives because we learnt so much . . .' His parents were English, very proper and very dignified. I was attracted to him mostly because he was a very good chef who was talented and focused and worked incredibly hard.

So after talking it over for ages with John, I decided to give our relationship a go. My parents met him and Mum wrote me a letter which said that while they had never really interfered in my life they wondered why a young man like that would be interested in me with three children, and that they didn't want to see me hurt.

Before John and I got together I sent Martin and Kirston to boarding school in Oamaru, which wasn't a happy experience for them, but at the time I thought I was doing the right thing. I was earning a bit more money by this stage and I wanted them to have both the discipline and educational advantages of boarding-school life.

We were still living in the A-frame house and I went to Todd's auction rooms in Invercargill and bought a baby pig to fatten at home. The first time the children came home in the school holidays I killed the pig and we had a party. Well, they hated me for killing their pet and also because I had started my relationship with John while they were away. They decided that John had encouraged me to kill the pig. Whichever way, I was in trouble.

Whenever the Braines went away on holiday I would manage the Esplanade for them and eventually they gave me a unit above the hotel where the kids and I lived for a few months.

By now, I was ready to leave Queenstown. I'd had enough of the social life and I didn't like the way the tourists were treated in the hotels. The people who came in on bus tours were generally known as 'loopies' because they travelled the loop from Christchurch to Te Anau and Queenstown, then back again to Christchurch. They didn't get to see what our country was about and most of the hotels herded them around like sheep. In the breakfast room at the Esplanade, some had paid a higher tariff and were allowed fruit and bacon while the others weren't, and you had to draft them. My idea was to let them all have whatever they wanted because you'd lose on some and win on others, but I wasn't allowed to change the system.

I also felt a growing need to create the kind of restaurant that I would like to eat in. I wanted to create a restaurant that was romantic; where a couple could go and have a lovely intimate dinner together; where a young guy could take a girl and introduce her to something exquisite. There was nowhere like that in the Alexandra, Clyde and Cromwell area. The one hotel in Alexandra required guests to be seated by a certain time; they were all called in together and if someone was late arriving the group had to order for them and the meal was put in the oven to stay warm.

Since my Dunstan House days I had yearned to do something with one of the old buildings Benjamin Naylor had built a hundred years earlier in Clyde, which were still owned by Ron and June Jackson. I thought, Wow, I know what I want to do. I could give people the opportunity to experience something new and beautiful. Step up! Get rid of your sausages and brown gravy from the packet! Welcome to a wonderful new world of food and dining out.

THERE WERE A
FEW POSSIBILITIES
FOR A NEW
VENTURE BUT
I KEPT COMING
BACK TO THE IDEA
OF MAKING A
TRULY ROMANTIC
RESTAURANT IN
RON AND JUNE
JACKSON'S
DISUSED GENERAL
STORE IN CLYDE.

5

NEW ZEALAND PROVENÇAL

I showed John what I envisaged and we talked about different scenarios before we decided we could do it together. I went to Clyde to talk to the Jacksons, and they agreed to rent the store to me for $50 a week.

Ron and June still owned the whole property I'd wanted to buy back in the mid-1960s — a beautiful big half-hectare block complete with eight buildings: a single-storey, five-bedroom stone house; Ben Naylor's former general store; a former bakery; smokehouses; a barn; stables; coach sheds; and a timber store with a central courtyard where three huge walnut trees gave shade. All of this was surrounded by high drystone walls. Naylor had built the property in 1863 and his general store had a broadly pitched gabled roof and at the back, a tiny lounge, a bedroom, a kitchen and another room with a fireplace. But it needed a huge amount of work because there was neither wiring nor plumbing and in places there weren't even wall-to-wall floors.

John and I rented a two-bedroom house on Fruitgrowers Road on the outskirts of Clyde and slept in a bus parked in the yard while the kids slept inside. However, I had done a terrible thing. I forgot to tell the kids at boarding school that we'd shifted, so it was only when I went to Cromwell to collect them off the bus from Oamaru and we headed back to Clyde that Kirston and Martin realised they had a new home. It didn't go down well. They still haven't quite forgiven me.

Ron and June couldn't imagine what John and I might do with the general store but they were very supportive, especially

Brendon, me, Kirston and Martin in
Clyde during the early Olivers days.

considering how much we inconvenienced them while we made
it ready for business. Their house was very close by and we had
to use their back drive for deliveries of building materials.
We worked on it for nearly a year, digging up the back yard to
lay sewerage pipes, cleaning the cobwebs and rat droppings out
of the crevasses in the internal stone walls, pulling up the rotten
floorboards and laying down demolition bricks over a concrete
pad. We took out walls and put in two enormous stone fireplaces.
Naylor's original mahogany shop counter became the bar on the
new mezzanine floor, which was reached by a beautiful polished-
wood staircase I had put aside for just such a purpose. The place
was wired throughout and we hauled in demolition doors and
windows, some of which I'd had in storage from my Dunstan
House days, and others I got from various contacts.

Olivers under construction

LEFT

The dust flying out the door as we were building Olivers.

BELOW

John in his other role as builder.

BOTTOM

The front of Olivers before a tourist ran into the verandah and demolished it.

The day Karl and I painted the front of Olivers red to prove to John he'd chosen the wrong colour.

Refurbishing the front.

Who *are* these young people?

We were working every daylight hour and half the night. John, I think it's fair to say, has terrible taste. He just wanted to get it finished so we could open and start making money, whereas for me it was a vision. I had an idea of how beautiful it was going to be and how it would work — people would want to come to this beautiful place and eat beautiful food. It would enrich people's lives and make couples have a longer, fuller, happier life together because they would be able to go out for dinner in a romantic place.

But there were a few bad patches getting to that point. We had stripped all the internal walls back to the old stone and there were other walls built of mud brick. While I was away one day John slathered a third of one of these huge walls with plaster. I was not pleased. I hadn't realised he didn't see things the way I did.

Luckily David Williams came in at that point and said, 'No,

LEFT & ABOVE

Photos taken for a tourism
promotion. The breakfast
room on the left.

OVERLEAF

One of the early stages of
the development of the
upstairs bar.

that's got to go. That *has* to go.' I knew in my heart that it had to go too, but it caused a lot of pain and anguish. It was a daunting job but the kids helped and we chipped off the plaster with hammers and chisels. To this day you can still see some white bits.

The 40-seat restaurant, when it was finished, was just as I had wanted it to be: the double walk-in fireplaces blazing with huge logs and red and green apples piled up on the enormous mantelpiece; all my old treasures from the estate auctions displayed on windowsills and tables; big Persian-style carpets laid over the brick floors; antique dressers festooned with massive arrangements of old-fashioned flowers and greenery; rosy lead-light lamp shades hanging from the forest-green ceiling; and old wooden tables covered in tartan cloths.

When we were making the alterations I was working intuitively. There weren't a lot of books and magazines around that showed what could be done and how to do it. When I read Peter Mayle's *A Year in Provence* some years later it made me smile because I'd been doing the same thing in Clyde, complete with all the problems in rebuilding, the struggles to get the stonework the way I wanted it, and having the joinery done so that everything looked as it might have done a hundred years before. And that's what made it work from the very beginning — the setting and ambience was authentic and it made people want to come in, sit in front of the fire and stay for a meal.

I had decided not to make any reference to Clyde's heritage in the name of the restaurant because I'd been disillusioned by the years I'd spent trying to persuade the locals, the government and the Historic Places Trust to take notice of the goldfields history that was physically disappearing. After considering any number of names we decided to call it Olivers, for three reasons. First, because I'm allergic to apostrophes, and second, because of the Dickensian allusions to food, as in 'I want some *more*'. Last, John's mother's maiden name had been Oliver. It was only later that I thought that wanting *more* still applied to my obsession with building on the history of Clyde and the Dunstan region.

We didn't do any market research to see if people were ready for something other than steak and chips or chicken Kiev. I just thought, I'm going to awaken this romantic feeling in people, that

Before and after.

every aspect of the atmosphere in which they eat their food, from the size and shape of the windows to the quality of the cutlery, is supposed to enhance their lives. And that's what I've been doing ever since. John, who is a genius in the kitchen, was able to combine ingredients and textures to create something different and remarkable every time.

We had decided that we would base our menus on simple, seasonal food that came from Otago. We had a small blackboard menu with tasty, quickly cooked local food that I eventually called 'New Zealand provençal' — meaning: from my province, my part of the country. We were among the first restaurants in New Zealand to serve Roger Belton's superb Pacific clams harvested from the coast around Otago and Bob and Sue Berry's Whitestone cheese from Oamaru. We always had Central Otago stone fruit, local vegetables and salad greens, and Otago-raised pork, beef and lamb. We had dishes like kidneys in a creamy mushroom sauce, tongue with Madeira sauce, venison spare ribs with a marmalade glaze and curried lambs' brains in a bread crust served with crisp bacon and a plum sauce. But of course, when the rabbiters came down from the hills with their freshly killed, thyme-fed rabbits we sent them away, explaining that we had a fridge full of the only rabbits you were allowed to serve in New Zealand at the time: shrink-wrapped albino-fleshed portions imported from China. The government was afraid that the rabbiters would leave a percentage of the rabbit population alive and available for future harvest if they were permitted to sell them to restaurants.

Still, we didn't intend to model our food on the cuisine of France. It wasn't till I went to France years later that I understood why people thought Olivers had a French influence — to me it was just traditional food cooked and presented with John's touch.

Not everyone liked it, of course. Some people wanted chips and eggs, or well-done meat and vegetables, whereas John cooked things very lightly as a matter of principle. A lot of the Central Otago people rejected what we had to offer. It's interesting that in later years I've had the same response from locals to the Moeraki and Oamaru restaurants.

At first, before we got a full licence at Olivers, we operated as a BYO. That really upset one of the local publicans and his patrons, who thought I was sending him broke. There was a big backlash. People coming out of the pub would pull their pants down and put their bottoms up against the window of my restaurant. They thought allowing people to bring their own wine to Olivers was illegal so a police officer tried to close me down one night. However, an important MP and a party of his friends were at the restaurant that evening, and after a bit of discussion the policeman left without charging me. There was a lot of ignorance about what we were doing but there were also a lot of people coming to the restaurant who were singing its praises and helping to build our name.

We didn't have a grand opening for Olivers; our clientele grew slowly so that we were already well established in the early 1980s when the German–New Zealand consortium Züblin-Williamson began building the Clyde dam on a seismic fault line above the town. (The dam is said to be an engineering feat, with its slip joint that is meant to withstand any earthquake. We'll see.) However, the dam construction bought us good business. In the evenings the construction workers were upstairs drinking in the bar while the German, French and Italian project managers were in the restaurant. The Germans especially, from the Züblin-Williamson company, were big clients and it was wonderful to have their patronage. They would click their fingers and call for cognac, which the floor staff thought was insulting, but it never worried me because having them there was exciting. It gave a certain European flavour to the restaurant right in the main street of Clyde.

The building and maintenance projects were never finished in the 20 years I was at Olivers. There was always something breaking down or falling apart or not in the right place and that was where John and I disagreed in our approach to the business. I was steeped in the history of Clyde; I had a profound understanding of where Naylor's store, and therefore Olivers, fitted into the 1860s goldfields, an understanding of the history of the hotels, the buildings, the pioneers and the broader picture of colonial New Zealand. It seems to me that the world is so crazy we need a sense of continuity from one generation to the next, and as far back as we can go. The aesthetics from times past are more beautiful than what we have today for the most part, and they soothe the soul. But John didn't see things that way. He had no concept of being in that beautiful building or understanding its history. He wanted to earn a lot of money and spend it on things other than the restaurant. In hindsight, given that he never had that historical perspective, he did very well to stay as long as he did.

In 1981 when we bought the whole property from the Jacksons for $120,000, it was a dream come true. In the first four years we'd had good numbers through the restaurant but owning the whole property gave us the opportunity to develop something that no one had seen in New Zealand before. There wasn't another group of buildings like this in the country.

Up to that point Olivers had given Clyde a huge boost. People were coming to the restaurant and wanted to stay overnight in the town rather than drive back to wherever they had come from. The motels and shops were busy. The motels provided continental breakfasts but the busier they got the less they wanted to be bothered doing breakfast, because they had the trade anyway. The same applied to Alexandra. At a moteliers' meeting one night I said to them, 'If you just take from the people and can't be bothered giving even a continental breakfast, I will build my own accommodation because I'm bringing them here for something really special and I want them to have the full experience of Central Otago.'

And even though I'd promised myself that I was going to focus on the business and not get back into promoting the area, as I had in the Dunstan House days, I could see that if I didn't do it there would be no real development of the potential I could see all around me. I started taking moteliers around to show them the places of interest in the district so they could at least tell their guests about the local history and point them to places they might like to explore.

At the end of 1980, just before we bought the property, the road was diverted from the middle of town so all highway traffic bypassed Clyde. I wrote letters for eight years to get a traffic light installed at the top of the hill to show the exit from the highway into the town but as a direct result of the bypass we lost $30,000 a year on our lunch trade. It was more obvious than ever that I needed to make Clyde a destination.

We renovated the original Naylor house next door to the restaurant, adding en suites to four bedrooms, decorating each room in a different colonial style and putting in French doors

This advertisement was designed and
illustrated by my daughter, Kirston. The
drawing of the baker in the top left was
to represent Michael Coughlin.

that led from each room into the courtyard. I used to say, only half-jokingly, that we converted the house because we didn't want to see people go after dinner on Saturday nights, and at midnight I'd invite people to breakfast on Sunday morning. Sometimes these meals went on all day. Before we had the accommodation, I'd had to stop doing that when John told me I'd have to cook the breakfasts myself.

Our next project was to set up little shops in the stables like a country marketplace to give the lodge and restaurant clientele a taste of the local talent and the locals an outlet for their wares. The shops — all of them converted horse stalls with their stable doors and resident pigeons — opened into the courtyard at the back of the restaurant. We had, at different times, a silversmith, a deli, antiques, leather clothing, confectionery, a fish market, fruit and vegetables, a soap factory, a tourism booking office and a bakery with our own in-house baker. At that point I started using brown paper bags as placemats because people wanted to take home the lovely bread they hadn't been able to finish. I also revived the old smokehouse so that we could cure our own meats. It was wonderful fun. People came from all over Otago to shop and have picnics on the lawn, and the complex began to attract media coverage.

The barn was already set up for catering and we were using it for functions where we served big joints of beef, cast-iron pots of ragout, braised rabbit and roasted lamb or mutton, and roast potatoes in more cast-iron pots. It was all laid out beautifully. I would trail branches from apple and crab apple trees down the centre of the tables, get out my collection of white linen napkins and bone-handled knives and silver-plated forks, and there would be big baskets of bread rolls to share.

A big part of Olivers' success in the early days came down to the relationship between John and me. John wasn't a very social person and I always tried to get him out of the kitchen to meet the customers but he would tend to gravitate to someone he knew. That was just the way he was, whereas I'd be all over the place enjoying my job.

We worked well together for the most part but we were both notoriously chaotic and quite often one or the other of us would lose the plot. If John was being a prat — outside laying bricks

Olivers courtyard

ABOVE

My parents at
Olivers.

RIGHT

The Chaîne des
Rôtisseurs dinner,
filmed by the Paul
Holmes show.

BELOW

Taste New Zealand
awards.

with his good chef's knife, for instance — I'd go out with a list of things he should have been doing and say, 'For fuck's sake, John, this needs ra-ra-ra, this, this, this and *now*!' And things would work. He'd come back inside, wash the knife, sharpen it up and start cutting steak.

On the other hand, John or someone else in the kitchen would always be banging on the bell to get me to come and take out an order I'd put through. Meanwhile I'd be in the dining room talking to someone or arranging table settings for a group who'd arrived without a booking. It used to be a standing joke — it was pointless ringing the bell for me to take a meal out and it was a constant argument between John and me. He'd say, 'Fleur, just, you know, go out! Host! Do *not* take care of tables,' because most times I'd flick an order into the kitchen and then get sidetracked. It used to drive everyone mad. I don't know why I'm using the past tense. I'm not much better these days.

Sometimes John would be rude to the patrons at the end of the night, by walking through the restaurant rattling the milk bottles all the way to the front door, or turning out most of the lights. Eventually we sorted it when I said I'd start the evening by being rude to all the patrons.

But John could cook anything. He'd look in your larder or fridge and then he'd deliver a mini-banquet to the table.

One of our best chefs during the Olivers' years was Michael Coughlin, who is the former owner of Dunedin's Bell Pepper Blues and now head chef at St Clair Beach Resort's Pier 24 restaurant. He is one of the most highly regarded chefs in New Zealand and he first came to work in the kitchen at Olivers when he was 19, having done his culinary training in the army and in the kitchen of a big tourist hotel in Queenstown.

John's whole approach to food was quite different to what Michael had been used to, having walked out of a kitchen run by the German chef Fritz Wagner where staff were physically abused every second day, having frozen legs of lamb thrown at them and being threatened with a ladle. Olivers didn't have the structure Michael was accustomed to, and there was always a sense that he was waiting for the other shoe to drop.

John cooked in a way that Michael hadn't seen before, such as

Martin's new colour scheme for the
signage and the front of the restaurant
looked great.

big roasted joints of beef, baked potatoes and interesting salads.
Michael had to learn to drop his adherence to classic dishes and
follow John's lead. John would cut Scotch fillets of beef and
marinate them in a red wine, onion and crushed mint. They were
chargrilled and he served them with a mint and mustard butter
sauce. This intrigued Michael, as it didn't fit into the *Répertoire de
la Cuisine*, the little bible of classic dishes that he knew through
and through.

The biggest seller at Olivers at the time was a crumbed chicken
breast stuffed with camembert cheese and Central Otago apricots.
This was the era of innovation where we were crumbing little wheels
of brie cheese, baking it in the oven and serving it with cranberry jelly
on a lettuce leaf as an entrée. It was a break from the shrimp cocktail.

Michael's first day happened to be Olivers' five-year anniversary.
He began by helping to assemble a champagne fountain John was
making out of a bath tub and a champagne magnum. We'd invited
all these people . . . it was one of our bigger parties. We took all the
guests to Waterfall Park and paid for them to go white-water rafting.

There were always adventures like that — we went white-water rafting for a staff party down the Kawarau River once and another time we went to Ohau Lodge for a ski party, then there was the time John chartered a friend's Cessna to go to see Dire Straits in Wellington. Most of the staff would drive up to Lake Hawea to go windsurfing after service on Saturday night; they'd camp on the back of a truck with bottles of champagne and eat Jimmy's Pies heated on the truck engine. They worked hard and they played really hard too.

Michael went off to work elsewhere after his first stint in our kitchen and then came back to run the bakery, which was a huge success. Olivers Barn had a second-hand 20-quart cake mixer and a hand pastry-break; he didn't even have a bun-divider initially so it was very labour intensive. Nearly everything had to be done by hand. Early in the morning on the day the bakery opened Michael had a display of beautiful Chelsea buns, different sandwiches and pies and wonderful loaves of bread. The artist Neil Driver, who lived around the corner, pulled up on his bike with his little son Josh on the back in a wee seat, and from thereon in he would show up every day.

Apart from the summer tourist season, the biggest trade all year round was from the Clyde dam site. Züblin-Williamson was on one side and the Ministry of Works on the other, so between them the bakery supplied a lot of food. They had 'tea huts' and 'tea boys', labourers assigned to collect orders and then come down and pick them up from the various places in Clyde. Michael would open the bakery doors at 6 am and the tea boys would be standing there with orders for dozens of pies, rolls and cream buns for the guys who had been working the night shift and wanted something to eat before going home. Then they needed food for tea breaks and lunches until 5 pm, when they'd be buying up for the night-shift crew again.

A couple of years later we converted the stables into 12 guest rooms in different styles. I had huge fun designing and decorating them. Each one opened onto the cobbled courtyard with urns of herbs, lavender, geraniums and roses on either side of the French doors. We'd had a lot of media coverage for the restaurant but once we opened the lodge, Olivers became something of a legend throughout New Zealand and we gained a lot of recognition for what we had achieved.

Olivers Decade

and to celebrate,

Fleur & John invite you to join the celebration, on

the lawn in CLYDE at 2.30pm.

on Saturday the 12th of December

Formalities will cease at 6.00pm and the true marathon

will begin.

an invitation to Karen + Alex

OLIVERS

Renowned for its fine food and warm surroundings
Available now is the very best in accommodation.
OLIVERS RESTAURANT AND LODGE
Main Street in Clyde
Phone (03) 449-2860. Fax (03) 449-2862

From the famous

Oliver's Restaurant

FILM CATERING

for the STARS

Olivers Film Unit, Catering Kitchen • Team
P.O. Box 38 CLYDE, 34 Sunderland Street CLYDE
JOHN BRAINE   Phone 0294 42860

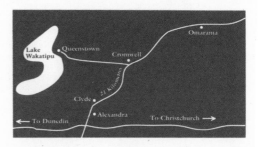

CLYDE . . .

One of the features on the Otago Goldfields Heritage Highway is a short turnoff from Highway 8 (Dunedin via Alexandra), 21km from Cromwell. The area is rich in gold mining history and those interested in New Zealand's colonial history will find much of interest.

*For reservations
inquiries and prices
please contact:*

Olivers Restaurant and Lodge

P.O. Box 38, Clyde, New Zealand
Telephone (03) 449-2860
Fax (03) 449-2862

Alan Brady, one of the pioneers of the Central Otago wine industry and founder of Gibbston Valley Wines, spent a lot of time at Olivers from the mid-1980s and throughout the following 10 years. What is now the Central Otago Wine Growers group used to meet at Olivers because it was a convenient halfway spot for the members. There were only four of them at that time and the association grew from those early meetings in 1985–86 when they were talking about how they were going to develop the industry.

ALAN BRADY

Fleur was and is a one-off. There's no one quite like her. She built Olivers at a time when theme bars and restaurants were coming into vogue around the country but they were all artificial — kind of Hollywood sets.

But Olivers, as I said in my book *Pinot Central,* was no fantasy conceived in the mind of an interior designer and executed by a team of set builders. This was Fleur. She created a genuine goldfields general-store atmosphere. She had a great respect for heritage and history and very little capital. She took this dilapidated building and imbued it with a vitality and a style that was unmatched in New Zealand at the time. She was quite amazing. She was a great host. She wore dark flowing gowns and she had a wonderful head of hair and she ruled over the place like a madam from the goldfields.

But Olivers wasn't just known as a place with great atmosphere, it was known for its food. She had this ability to create a regional essence in all the food she created. Rabbit, thyme and apricots were prominent ingredients in a lot of her dishes. Food writers raved about it.

Ours is a very celebratory industry. We mark occasions and we're very aware of history and all the traditions that go with wine. One of them is that you celebrate harvest and you celebrate successes. We've held the annual Feraud dinner since the early 1990s and the first ones were held at Olivers.

But one of Fleur's big handicaps was always a lack of capital, and Olivers was horrendously expensive to maintain. There were all these old buildings and constant repairs and renovations going on. But after Fleur left no one else was able to recapture what she had created at Olivers.

LEFT

Mike Hood.

RIGHT

This painting, by
Neil Driver, caused
some people
to cancel their
bookings.

They held their meetings in the Olivers garden and we'd always put on elaborate platter lunches. They ate in the shade of a big walnut tree during the summer months. The yard was cobbled and you entered either through the restaurant or through big iron gates, and there were silkie white Bantams strutting around. Alan would say it was like stepping from New Zealand into rural France. He would bring people down from Queenstown for lunch just for them to experience the atmosphere.

Mike Hood was our regular musician at Olivers for many years. He came to dinner at the restaurant one night with friends, and introduced himself to me at the end of the evening, saying, 'If you ever need any music, give me a call.' He was a closet guitar player at that point and had never performed in public, but he didn't tell me that. I rang him the next week and said, 'We've got a function down here, would you like to play at it?'

He had 30 songs he could play all the way through, one guitar,

a really old microphone and no PA. It was a bit of a nightmare because he had to plug into the house system that we put the tapes through. But he played the set twice that day and after that he became our most frequent musical act other than Gwen and Gloria.

Gwen and Gloria were an amazing duo who came out of am dram in Alex. Gwen, who was a prolific and talented composer of beautiful music, played the piano, usually with a cigarette placed between two fingers, and Gloria, who was larger than life and a consummate entertainer, would walk around the room playing the double bass and singing songs from World War Two.

Mike would play every third weekend or so and eventually he became a regular. He'd take off from time to time to get away from what he called the bedlam — that goes with the way I run things.

Mike says I thrive on chaos. He reckons part of my routine is that if everything is running smoothly — the seating plan's arranged and everyone's coming at the right time — I'm bored instantly, so I find a new problem to solve. In fact, it's like a jigsaw puzzle — I have to find where the casual customers fit. For instance, even though the plan said we were doing 60 covers, by the end of the night we've done 93. It's what I've always done best: meeting the challenge of seating everybody, getting to

ABOVE

A van Geldermalsen family
gathering, with the model in
the painting on page 121 at
bottom left.

BELOW

The kitchen at Olivers.

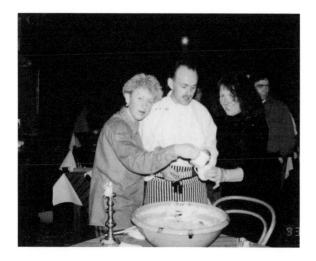

The dream team
— Cindy, chef
Albert and me.
Note the
little finger!

know them, making sure they have a good time.

There were nights at Olivers that seem to have almost found a place in New Zealand folklore. In reality, the most raucous ones happened when I was away, which wasn't that often. John would really play up if I wasn't there to keep an eye on things. Mike tells about the night when he was offered some chunky homemade chocolates, which he accepted . . . After playing a few more songs Mike realised he couldn't walk. His legs wouldn't work. He cottoned on when he found out the chocolates were stuffed with crushed marijuana leaves. Apparently the staff were handing the things around willy-nilly except for one corner of the restaurant, where the head of police in Alexandra was sitting. He was the only one who didn't get any, while there were people falling about laughing all over the place.

When I arrived back from wherever I'd been, they all scuttled for cover. I took a look around the room and asked, 'What's going on here?' and they were all giggling and laughing and trying to look casual.

I remember another night when most of the kitchen staff ate some hash cookies that someone had brought in. They got the munchies and ate all the food that was supposed to go out for my birthday supper. There was very little left and they had to spread it out. I was furious but all they could do in the kitchen was giggle.

We had a regular procession of performers and musicians through Arts Council tours, and there were legendary performances from the likes of Hello Sailor and a particularly memorable night with Julie Felix and the greater Dunedin folk scene. The Topp Twins were there a lot, Sam Hunt, Tim Shadbolt and Gary McCormick too; Herbs played on the lawn; The Warratahs were there all the time. We hosted the best of New Zealand music and we loved doing it.

WAYNE MASON

The Warratahs first went to Olivers around the time of the Gold Guitars in Gore about May '87, and we kept going back there until 1993–94 when we broke up the band. The venue was a new experience for us — a big stone building with stone fireplaces and a grand piano.

We usually played in the restaurant — they'd
move the tables around and we'd stick ourselves
in a corner and play. Fleur was a character and
she had a real feel for the history of the town.
I was really into trains and we used to have a lot
of conversations about the Otago Central Line
and its retention.

John was a very cool dude and the food was
amazing. It was more avant-garde than the
restaurants we ate at while we were on the road.
It had a more European feel to it. Fleur's son,
Martin, is a really great sculptor and she had
artworks all over the place so she had a foot in
the art camp as well.

It was one of the best gigs in New Zealand.
We ate off the menu and sat around afterwards
in front of the fire, drinking wine and talking and
laughing. It wasn't a bad way to live. We used to
hang out in the kitchen because the place felt
like home. I think we even helped out doing the
dishes once or twice! The most interesting thing I
found there was the social interaction. Fleur used to
get a lot of dam workers drinking at the bar upstairs
but her restaurant clientele were big foodies and
into their wine; they obviously knew their stuff.
She surrounds herself with interesting people.

Illustrious Energy

LEFT

The contacts I made during the filming of *Illustrious Energy* sowed the seeds of the beginning of the Goldfields Heritage Trust. Geeling Ng and me at a special screening of the film in Dunedin to launch the trust. The launch was held at Mr Eddie Chin's nightclub.

ABOVE

The *Illustrious Energy* film set, Dunstan House at rear.

LEFT

My daughter Kirston on set in the opium den.

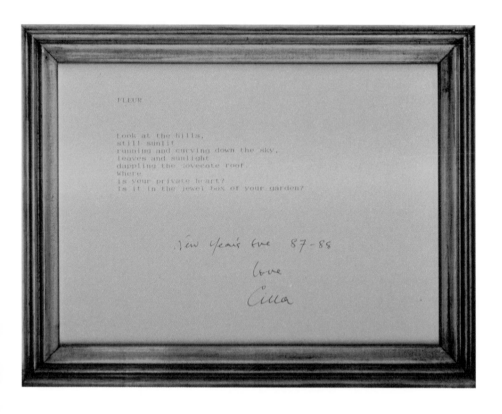

FLEUR

Look at the hills,
still sunlit
running and curving down the sky,
leaves and sunlight
dappling the dovecote roof.
Where
is your private heart?
Is it in the jewel box of your garden?

New Year's Eve 87-88
love
Cilla

ABOVE

Friends at the launch of Olivers Lodge
to travel agents in Auckland.

Because I was always so busy and had a commitment to perfection, I was the person who didn't go on holiday; I wasn't being a martyr because I loved working and I was the one who said what we were and what we did, so that's how it had to be. But the rewards were that I could have beautiful bath fittings and lovely wallpaper and beautiful linen; I could buy paintings. I bought the works of South Island artists wherever possible: Elizabeth Stevens, my son Martin Sullivan, Peter Cleverley, Ian Shanks, Janny van Geldermalsen and Jane Evans.

TIM SHADBOLT

I was elected Mayor of Waitemata City in 1983 and was promptly sued by the opposition mayoral candidate, my own council and my CEO, so suddenly I was employing five lawyers to fend off these libel suits. A mayor's honorarium at that time was about $18,000 so I had to get out on the road and earn some funds to pay my lawyers, because if you're bankrupt you can't hold public office.

I was doing a variety of performances throughout the country. Sometimes they'd be debates — I did a series with Tom Scott and Gary McCormick and we'd take on three local identities. Then there were the stand-up comedy shows, the corporate gigs when I'd be the after-dinner guest speaker and the shows when we'd combine poetry, music and comedy.

A lot of these shows took me to Queenstown, which at that time was quite isolated. Wanaka hadn't been developed and while I would also perform in Dunedin and Invercargill there weren't any other towns in the Queenstown area with a population that would sustain these sort of events. But then there was this shining little outpost down in Clyde, and the opportunity to do two shows in the region, which was great. And, of course, Olivers!

When you're on the road a lot as a performer you're usually put in the same category as cleaners and bar staff. There are never any changing rooms to speak of and never any meals. You'd buy a pie at the garage or something. Suddenly here was this owner-operator who actually appreciated her performers and artists, who would give us food and a little room to organise ourselves in. It was just such a nice point of difference. We'd go out of our way to get a gig there and I'd recommend it to other performers. I did shows with Hammond Gamble, Sam Hunt and Gary McCormick, all the usual suspects, and we'd sing Fleur's praises everywhere we went. And she was always so charming and the hospitality was just superb. So was the food, and the secret there, I think, was in the spices and sauces and the presentation.

I often wondered what attracted people most to Olivers. Was it the food — that it was so superior to anything you'd get anywhere else in the region, including Queenstown — or was it Fleur's personality and all the razzmatazz that went with her? We felt like we were in the vanguard of something new and different. It all seemed so exciting.

In the early days Neil Driver was a struggling artist in Clyde
— he's still there — and his wife Christine was a schoolteacher.
They couldn't afford to eat out very often so we traded meals as
part payment for some of his paintings. Sadly, he had trained as
an accountant, which didn't allow him to eat, drink and be merry
too often — so I couldn't get a painting every week. I wished he
could have been more like Toulouse-Lautrec.

All this didn't mean that I had lots of money, but I was making
a beautiful place and beautiful people were coming.

John had made good contacts through David Williams and was
catering for film companies soon after we bought the Olivers block
in 1981. The kitchen staff were prepping meals at Olivers and John
was also cooking on set, so together with Michael's bakery items
we were sending vanloads of food out to the sets of films like *Race
for the Yankee Zephyr, Battletruck, Willow* and *Illustrious Energy*.
The cast and crew of these films were at Olivers for meals and it
was wonderful fun having them there. The actress Geeling Ng,
who was David Bowie's 'China Girl' in the music video, was a lead
actress in the 1986 film *Illustrious Energy* and I still have photos of
the two of us in an old Cobb & Co coach.

Right from the beginning, after we'd been open for only a few
months, I was back into promoting the local heritage in a big way.
In 1985 I organised a celebration to mark the arrival of the first
Cobb & Co coach at the Dunstan goldfields from Dunedin 123
years earlier. I borrowed the coach from the Lawrence Museum
and had it trucked to Clyde, where it sat on the lawn outside
Olivers. We had live music, food stalls, pony-cart rides for the
senior citizens of the town, a fashion parade and a guided tour of
the streets of Clyde. It was part of my campaign to celebrate the
local heritage and we did it for the next two or three years but it
was too hard to sustain it alone. At least the seeds were sown for
the Goldfields Heritage Trust.

Running Olivers was one of the biggest pleasures in my life.
We knew we were having an impact when we began to win awards
for the restaurant and lodge complex. From the early '80s we won,
at different times, the Listener–Montana Wines Best Provincial
Restaurant award, a New Zealand Historic Places Trust award for
restoration of the buildings, a New Zealand Tourism (NZT) Award

My father on the Cobb & Co coach,
travelling through the goldfields,
St Bathans.

for the best boutique accommodation, a personal NZT award for
enterprise in tourism, an inaugural Equal Opportunity Employer
award and I was made an Officer of the New Zealand Order of Merit.
We also won any number of food industry awards. I imagined all
this recognition gave us credibility in the wider sense but it never
made any difference to the locals.

At the same time I was always coming up with new ventures
attached to the restaurant and lodge. The Blue Bottle Cidery that
we set up produced house cider for several seasons made from
apples we had personally wassailed each year on a cold winter's
night. Sometime in August a crowd of us would go out to the
orchard where we got our apples to wake up the tree spirits by
yelling and hooting and banging on pots with metal spoons,
before pushing cider-soaked bread into the crooks of the branches
and throwing capfuls of cider over the branches to placate the
wakened spirits. Then we'd dance around the tree, singing

Mrs Fleur Sullivan surveys the destroyed museum piece she found lying in the Clyde tip this week.

Dumping of museum piece raises ire

By Megan Mavor

Clyde. — A former Clyde Museum piece, an old seed crusher, was disposed of in the Clyde tip last week, and a Clyde resident is objecting to the disposal procedure.

The objectors, Mrs Fleur Sullivan, who retrieved the destroyed crusher from the tip, said she could not believe how a museum committee could dispose of a piece of "folk craft" in the way they did.

"I want a complete investigation into the affairs of the museum committee and their procedures," Mrs Sullivan said.

The chairman of the Clyde Museum committee, Mr Evan Blanch, said he was disappointed in the way some of the committee members had acted over the matter. He said the whole museum committee was not consulted about the disposal of the ice.

The members of the committee who allegedly disposed of the item did not want to comment to the *Otago Daily Times* yesterday.

Mr Blanch said the matter would be discussed at the next meeting of the committee.

RIGHT

The old seed crusher before it was thrown away. I was so upset about its disposal that I closed the restaurant for the day.

traditional wasailling songs. Wassailed apple trees are so much more productive than those that have been left alone all winter. The ceremony also gave the staff a bit of a lift. I often hear from people who worked with us in those days, and they tell me that this kind of thing hardly ever happens in other places they've worked.

One of the really wonderful things about it was that Olivers was open to all and you could trust everybody. At those parties on the lawn . . . everybody was honest, everybody paid their bill and everybody looked after what was there. We didn't lock anything and it was never a problem.

In the early days it was always a source of some confusion and sadness for me that so few of the people in the smaller towns of Central embraced what Olivers had to offer but the locals who were brave enough to come in were soon converted.

Because we wanted our guests to see the best of what the region had to offer we made connections with tourism operators all over Central and put groups together for horse treks, fishing, shooting, gold fossicking, garden tours and photographic outings. We were lucky that we had customers from Queenstown and Wanaka because there wasn't really anybody in the region doing what we were doing. So when the mountain was closed with cloud, when river guides couldn't take people out, when fishing guides couldn't take people on the rivers, they all brought them over to Olivers where they sat around the great big fire with a grappa bowl. We got a lot of work that way. It meant that tour operators were able to say, 'Oh well, you can't do what you've come all this way to do but we'll take you over to Olivers in Clyde and you're guaranteed a great time.'

However, building the Olivers complex, running the business and dealing with the finances and money worries was never, never easy. The work that we did, the maintenance, the heating of the place — I would never change what we had, but we did it by the skin of our teeth and we were constantly re-inventing ourselves.

There were also things outside our control that made it harder, as they did for everyone in the country. There were escalating petrol prices, the economic downturn, the crisis in the farming sector and the stock-market crash. I simply didn't realise the effect this was having on John but when he left and it looked like I might lose the business too, I felt as if the world was crashing down around me.

I DIDN'T REALISE IT AT THE TIME BUT JOHN WAS PREPARING HIS EXIT FOR 18 MONTHS BEFORE HE LEFT ON 8 DECEMBER 1992.

6

STARS AND SCARS

He had become obsessed with the need to go further and further, faster and faster, increasing turnover by adding more accommodation suites. His seemingly frantic state allowed him to accomplish impossible feats of construction and maintenance, such as rebuilding a bathroom in a day, cutting through stone walls alone or standing on the lodge's roof pouring on buckets of paint and sweeping it on with a broom.

At the same time, he was leaving the running of the kitchen to the junior chefs and it began to show in the food we were serving.

And then there was the other behaviour.

Over the years, on my rare nights away from the restaurant, John would bed his favourite staff member of the moment. I would know whose turn it had been by their newfound sense of ownership of him and the restaurant. There are always women who will be attracted to someone in a position of authority and men willing to take advantage of that fact. As far as John and I were concerned I didn't take it personally, except that we had agreed that if either of us wanted to change the nature of our relationship, we'd discuss it openly. In the big scheme of Olivers it didn't matter too much to me.

I had long since grown tired of John's constant need for affirmation and approval. My biggest priorities were my personal responsibilities and the demands of the business. I never thought that John would give up his lifestyle of off-road vehicles, wind-surfing and trips to the islands, and the friends who shared that

ABOVE LEFT & LEFT

Winter at Olivers.

ABOVE

The wall I had
built after John
left. The most
magnificent in
Central Otago.

way of life, for just one waitress, but he did.

This woman had money and a business; after he left, Marilyn Annan, our admin assistant, and I went into our files on the computer and found a spreadsheet detailing her business activities, which showed that a loan John had taken with a finance company was being paid back out of her business account.

I was almost numb with shock. The crisis came when we began to unravel all the financial details and found that the true extent of the business's debt was close to one million dollars. The regular accounts hadn't been paid for months; there were demand notices from the power and telephone companies and there was court action pending from the Inland Revenue Department. I also felt it was my duty to let this woman know about John's state of mind so I booked myself on a flight to Reporoa where she lived. My intention was to ask her to take the pressure off John, but to allow him to sort out our business affairs so we could sell Olivers. I said she could have him back at the beginning of the financial year, or alternatively buy him out. That turned out to be quite an adventure. Someone on the plane mistook me for a woman who had been missing in Marlborough and told the air hostess. The pilot then contacted the police in Queenstown. The police checked with the airline counter to confirm if it was me on the plane and asked for my next of kin. They then rang John to confirm that I was headed for Reporoa. So my visit to explain the circumstances that I found myself in was no longer a surprise.

I had been afraid for some time that John was on the verge of a complete breakdown, so in September 1992 I had arranged to lease out the restaurant arm of the business. I wanted to take the pressure off him, on the understanding that he and I could then concentrate on the marketing of the lodge, developing the barn and maintaining the gardens.

The lessees were to pay me a percentage of their turnover, but as it turned out, that meant they had no incentive to put in the hours after they'd reached their target. Within a few weeks it was obvious it wasn't going to work.

We had won the Tourism New Zealand Top Boutique Lodge award and any number of other industry and tourism awards, and people were continuing to flock to Olivers. The lodge was full seven days a week but the lessees would only take restaurant bookings on five or six days. And to be fair, why should they work long hours, seven days a week? They could make as much as they needed to in six days. The big picture was not their problem.

But the point was that the restaurant was still the primary part of the business. It provided most of the income that paid for the maintenance of the whole property: the roofs, the creeper growing under the spouting, the old stone walls, all the plumbing, all the heating, miles and miles of underground copper pipes, the big boiler, the laundry. In terms of infrastructure, nothing worked independently of the restaurant. The lodge kitchen was not equipped to cope with a full house, so everything depended on the service from the restaurant kitchen, chillers and freezers.

The lessees didn't want to pay for live music, they could cut their overheads by reducing staff if they wished and take only as many diners as they could handle comfortably.

I was in a state of blind panic trying to work out how I was going to make it work. People were arriving because of the publicity around the latest award, we were on the brink of realising everything we had been working towards and it was all falling to pieces. Although John had been there, he had been virtually absent for 18 months.

The crisis came the day when a party from the New Zealand Tourism Board, as well as the broadcaster John Hawkesby and his wife, had booked in for an evening meal but the bar and restaurant were closed. I was almost beyond functioning rationally, sitting at my work table, seriously considering the possibility of taking my longest, sharpest knife and sinking forward onto it, when there was a rap at the window. Michael Coughlin and his wife Mari Anne peered in. They had been visiting family in Cromwell and decided to drop by, not knowing that John had left. When I gave my semi-hysterical account of what was happening Michael took over.

He asked if I had any money so I opened the drawer and gave him about $100 in loose notes. They both headed to the Alexandra New World and came back with a fillet of beef, tomatoes and mozzarella, fresh local berries and other ingredients for a simple three-course meal. Michael cooked in the lodge kitchen while Mari Anne, who had been a waitress at Olivers, served at the breakfast-room table and I played host. We got through it and I'll

Clyde   Central Otago NZ.

**Olivers
lodge and
restaurant**

ABOVE FAR LEFT

The front of restaurant.

BELOW FAR LEFT

The barn with my winter's
supply of stacked wood.

ABOVE

The lodge kitchen.

RIGHT

These roses are from the
original garden.

BELOW

The lodge breakfast room.

be forever grateful to them. Now it was absolutely essential that I found a way to get that restaurant back so I could start paying off the debt.

It wasn't easy. Someone who can't be named publicly financed the services of a lawyer to negotiate the dissolving of the lease. The understanding was that if it could be resolved at that level I would be given the service free of charge, but if it were to go to court I'd have to pay the costs. Persuading the couple to relinquish the lease wasn't easy for them or me; I'd never have believed I could summon such powers of manipulation but it had to be done. When I put my feet on the floor every morning I was walking into a nightmare, trying to hold it all together. When there's talk about how many people have failed at Olivers since I was there, I always say that we could have failed as well.

Some time later a fruitgrower held his daughter's wedding function at Olivers and various friends — musician Mike Hood, local pharmacist Trevor Sutherland, lawyer Ray Blake, florist Gail Banks, stonemasons Bob and Steve, and teacher Chris Fowle — were in the barn carving meat and putting the dishes together. I remember driving to the bank with a large cheque on the Monday thinking it would've been the end of the world if I hadn't done that wedding and been paid. The $500 tip to shout the staff for a job well done made us heady with pride.

Once I had the restaurant back in early January 1993 I then had to find a chef and a full complement of kitchen staff. It was a matter of making do with whatever kitchen staff and chefs I could find until French chef Gilbert Prevost arrived later in the year.

Either side of Gilbert's time at Olivers I had a succession of madmen and incompetents running the kitchen. There was the control freak who refused to follow my recipes and wanted to do everything his way. It certainly helped me to understand him when he told me that he'd not long been married when his wife left him. She didn't tell him she was going but she stabbed his set of chef's knives through the top layer of their wedding cake right up to the hilt and left it on the kitchen table. I've always imagined the handles glinting like macabre candles.

Then there was the profligate Irishman who was a treasure but almost brought the restaurant to its knees financially; there was

the guy who was always drunk by 10 am; the one who used to dress
up as an air hostess; the one who ran off overseas with one of the
waitresses; and the ones that were just surly and nasty. It went on
and on. They would get their own back at me for telling them what
to do by serving badly prepared, badly cooked food with no
thought of what it was doing to the business. Of course there were
also the chefs who were calm and competent, but no one stayed for
very long because Clyde is not the centre of the universe as far as
young people and chefs are concerned. We survived only because
of the ambience in the restaurant. We still had a beautiful setting:
the fires, the music, the bar upstairs, the beautiful lodge and the
beautiful rooms. And even though there was no one else in the
region doing really good food it was heartbreaking for me to have
to settle for as good as I could get on the day. The biggest hurdle to
jump was the number of staff and suppliers who thought I was
going to go broke anyway — so why bother. But I heard my dad
saying, 'Don't let the bastards beat you.'

Gilbert's arrival felt like the cavalry coming to the rescue.
Because he is French, his training, his passion for food and his
work ethic made me realise that this was the person I had been
trying to attract to the restaurant all the time. I was able to be
proud of the restaurant again and front it with confidence.
Even so, while the business, and consequently my life, improved
phenomenally after Gilbert arrived it was no easier for him to find
the right people to work with than it had been for me because so
few wanted to live in a small town. When Gilbert, who has always
been a gypsy, left late in 1995, I carried on as best I could.

The debt diminished as the guests kept coming. The reviews,
magazine articles and television programmes featuring Olivers
continued to appear over the next couple of years. We now had
a high standard to maintain.

Peta Mathias stayed for three days in 1995 with a film crew
to do a programme on the food of Central Otago for the Taste
New Zealand segment of TVNZ's *Town & Country*. She was funny
and gorgeous and we talked about the joys and pitfalls of being
a restaurant proprietor; she had owned one in France a few years
before. Later she posted me a badge that read 'If you catch me
buying a restaurant, shoot me!'

IF YOU CATCH ME BUYING A RESTAURANT!

SHOOT ME

Olivers courtyard
with Peta Mathias.

...e blonde bombshell. She's the best show in
...ly show in town. We drove from Gibbston
:, where Chris, Laurence, Barrie, John and I
...ver's Lodge for three nights while filming our
. By this time it was becoming suspiciously
...outh Islanders are
...n North Islanders.
...on of sympathique is
...ociable, to be nice,
...the most accurate
...th.
...s, Peta,' scoffed my
...nders are dour,
...aginative.'
...o be so. I'm sorry. I
...g of which I had not
...· else in the country
...Aucklanders. They think they're all money,
...l, no culture, superficial high-flyers. What a
...if we have the most beautiful harbour in the
...if the sun shines all the time (except when it's
...it that we're so good looking? Let's be mature
...e disagrees with me, I will stomp out of the
...or.
...love the South Island. Fleur started off on a
...en we straggled into her restaurant she

...utiful. We need a bit of that around here.'
...ressed,' I replied. 'Under this makeup is a

...elves in our cool, large house. We had the
...elves with en-suited bedrooms, lounge and
. we pleased. While the others drank Speights
...tables, I went for a little evening walk around
...nd were lots of churches and lots of foxgloves.
...ecred in a shop window and came face to face
...ed me in to peruse her latest acquisition, the
...l. She's gradually doing it up to live in, and
...ice there in a cocoon of maroon walls, velvet

PETA AND FLEUR DISCUSS HAIRDOS.

To Fleur
with lots of love
Peta
xx

CENTRAL OTAGO ■ 88

One of the high points at Olivers was the day we received the
first delivery of Alan Brady's Gibbston Valley Wines and I could go
outside and write on the blackboard 'Food *and Wine* of the region.'
Very shortly afterwards we also had Rippon wines from Wanaka
and Black Ridge wines from Conroys Gully. It felt like my region
had come of age.

❖

Then there was the return of Henry Blofeld.

Years before, when the world-famous English cricket commentator had eaten at the restaurant, he had fallen in love with me. I suspect he made a habit of falling in love with women when he was away from home but it was really funny because when I first met him I had no idea who he was. I know absolutely nothing about cricket.

He told me all about his estate in England and how he shot grouse, deer and partridge, and that he made the best bread sauce in England. He said he would like to cook me a meal. I let him know that I was not free to return his sentiments and Henry said to me that if ever, ever I changed my mind I was to ring his London club, Boodles. He could be reached anywhere in the world within 24 hours and he would be in touch.

One night, not long after John had left, I was drowning my sorrows with a few friends who were commiserating with me. I was wailing, 'Oh, Henry Blofeld loves me, please ring Henry Blofeld! Tell him I can't wait to taste his bread sauce.'

This would have been at about 11 pm, so Marilyn, the office manager, rang Boodles in London. She got an escort agency on her first attempt so she tried to sober up, and when she got through to the right number she said, 'I have a message for Henry Blofeld.' They said, 'We haven't seen Mr Blofeld for some time', followed by, 'Oh, here comes Mr Blofeld now.' He took the call. Marilyn said that she was Fleur Sullivan's secretary so he asked to speak to me . . . and I was in the background saying, 'No, no, no . . .' I don't know what she said I was doing but he said he was coming over soon to do some commentating, but that he was going to India first and he wanted me to join him there.

After that, while he was in India or Sri Lanka or somewhere, he kept ringing up. One night he rang and whoever took the message said I was too busy to come to the phone. We were really busy. So he'd said to the girl, 'Tell her to get a pen and paper and come to the phone in 20 minutes.' When he rang back he said, 'I've held the plane up, I'm in the middle of a riot and your girl tells me you're busy!' He asked me to join him overseas for the tour.

Off to cook at the annual chef's dinner in
Auckland for the restaurant association.

I said to him, 'But you've married again, haven't you?' and he said something about being in a state of limbo just now. I replied, 'I'm not coming over there and hiding in the wardrobe, Henry!'

I didn't go but he did visit me on his next cricket trip to New Zealand. It was a delightful relief after all the stress of recent times. He wrote a newspaper column and mentioned me and whenever he was commentating he'd find a way to refer to Olivers.

When he arrived in Clyde to stay at the lodge he told me that he'd lost all his money as a Name for Lloyds of London and he'd had to sell his huge library so he was a bit miserable. He sat in my garden for a few days and then he offered to do an after-dinner talk. I thought, God, who'd want to listen to Henry?

What did I know? So many people came to the restaurant when they knew Henry Blofeld was there — they found him totally fascinating. Erina and Terry McLean, old friends from Queenstown days and the parents of Aaron McLean, whose photographs appear in this book, came over because they adored Henry. And he said to them, 'Well, Fleur seems to be the only person who doesn't think I'm funny. I'm much sought after as an after-dinner speaker and I'm offering to do it for her but she doesn't think that anybody will come.'

Erina and Terry had a talk to me and said, 'Go on. You've got to do it.' Word quickly spread and we were full in no time at all. Henry gave an amazingly funny talk. I can't remember now how much money we made but it was a good night's takings. It certainly gave me a boost.

He was lovely with children, too. By this time my daughter Kirston had a beautiful four-year-old daughter, Ruby. I remember watching Henry read with Ruby in the courtyard one day. She had a pop-up book with castles and dungeons and said to him, 'You'll be the knave.' Henry said, 'Oh no, I intend to be the king of the castle.' Ruby insisted that he couldn't be, and when he asked why, she replied, 'Because I've got the drawbridge.' Henry laughed and conceded defeat.

While he was sitting in the courtyard, people would walk up to him and start chatting, and they'd suddenly realise who they were talking to. They'd exclaim, 'You're Henry Blofeld, aren't you?' Henry would reply, 'Get me a glass of good red wine and I'll tell you about the time . . .'

SAM HUNT

Olivers was special, one of the high temples of the performance circuit for me. There are certain venues that have always been there and have got a history, like the Gluepot in Auckland. Fleur was a newcomer in the early '80s but you felt that she had always been there.

My first impression of Fleur was one of an
incredibly truthful person. Straight to the
bulls-eye. And of course colourful and delightful.
One of those people who make you believe in
words like *consecration*.

When tours were planned throughout the '80s
and '90s there were certain places that you liked,
so you made sure the person who was putting the
tour together would give you a few days off at that
point. Having been going flat out for a week doing
a show each night I would most definitely have a
few days off both at Clyde and later at Moeraki.

Fleur's like — to quote Baxter speaking of
someone else — those who:

gave the space for art
Time for the re-shaping of the heart.

Fleur was certainly a high point of the highway
life with her hospitality and her originality
and her colour and her uniqueness. When you
are living on the highway you remember certain
places — will they water the horses well?
And she watered the horses really well.

And speaking of horses, I always used to quote
the Baxter line to Fleur — The barman:

won the trots at Clyde
the day that Concrete Grady died.

She's got this ability that you come across in
other art forms — to make something that's very
difficult seem so simple. The Italians have a word
for it — *sprezzatura* — and she has that ability.
Denis Glover used to say, 'Don't forget, Sambo, the
simple poems are the hard ones to write but they're
the ones to write.' Well, Fleur is a living example of
that way of thinking and that way of living.

Henry was one of hundreds of national and international visitors we hosted at Olivers over the years. When I give public talks I'm often asked to name them and I always say I'd have to go through most of the musical, literary, art, film, political, media and sporting identities in the country as well as some notable people from abroad.

Sam Neill, the actor, was a regular patron and I always admired his charm, good looks and impeccable dress sense. One evening he booked in for a meal and overnight accommodation in the lodge and told me he'd have to leave before 7 am the following day. I said we'd get him a decent breakfast before he left. When I came in early the next morning to make sure everything was all right I found him sitting in the lounge looking a bit distressed. It turned out he'd locked his keys in the boot of his rental car the night before. It was not much after 7 am; there were no rental-car agencies that would be open at that time of day but I had a thought. I said, 'I know a couple of guys who are used to getting into locked cars. Do you want me to call them?' He said he did so I made a phone call and we went out into the street to wait for the rescue squad. They came around the corner, one Pakeha with a shaved head and wearing camouflage gear, the other Maori with dreadlocks and a long hand-knitted coat in Rasta colours. They nodded to us, then one of them pointed up to the highway and muttered, 'What the fuck is *that*?' Sam and I turned around to see what he was talking about and by the time we looked back, the front door of the car was open, the boot was up and the stereo was blasting. The other one said, 'Looks like some dirty hua has busted your window, mister.' Sam thanked them appropriately, got in the car and drove off.

Politicians of all persuasions dined at Olivers at one time or another. The day we catered the huge party to celebrate the completion of the Clyde dam project, I waited on the table with Prime Minister Jim Bolger and his wife, Joan. They said one of their sons had been best man at a wedding at Olivers four years earlier and had told them they should make a point of coming to stay at the lodge. It was nice that someone as busy as the prime minister could still remember what his son had been doing four years ago.

I also remember the evening when what seemed like half the little kids in Clyde started racing through the doors of the restaurant.

HEARTLAND HABITS

BY FLEUR SULLIVAN

At five, I remember watching an ample nun, sleeves rolled up, habit tucked into her belt, kneading bread on a scrubbed wooden table in an old cellar kitchen under St Joseph's Convent in Oamaru. The image has never left me and ever since I have been fascinated by food, kitchens, utensils, herbs, and the traditions of good food production. I will happily read, buy and borrow cookbooks and daydream

chosen are a seared venison with pickled blackberry sauce, and a simple plum pudding with a caramel sauce. They match the grand scale of Central Otago in midwinter.

VENISON WITH A SPICED BLACKBERRY PICKLE SAUCE
1 fillet venison (1-1.5kg)
8 slices fat bacon
4 sage leaves
1 tsp chopped thyme
½ tsp each oregano, marjoram, rosemary
2 bay-leaves
1 cup vegetable oil
juice of 1 lemon
salt and pepper
450g Stonehouse Spiced Blackberry Pickle
¼ cup red wine or port
 Wipe the venison with a clean cloth, lard with fat bacon, or tie the bacon on with string

over them for hours – then boil an egg.
 Another early food memory is of eating huhu grubs as a seven-year-old. My mother showed me the grubs in an old log and told me how the Maori ate them. Later I cooked them on a friend's mother's coal range.
 Many years later I moved to Clyde, and started a bed and breakfast and antique business in the old Dunstan Hotel. My next venture was setting up Olivers Restaurant and Lodge across the road. Winning the *Listener* Montana Best Provincial Restaurant Award in 1989 and 1990 confirmed my beliefs about making the most of a region's foods. My goal has been to combine these ingredients into simple food, with an emphasis on venison, rabbit, stonefruits, nuts, and seasonings such as wild thyme. The recipes I have

and tuck in fresh rosemary sprigs. Mix the chopped herbs, oil and lemon juice, and season well, and marinate the meat for at least 2 hours, turning occasionally. Heat a ridged skillet and sear the meat, turning and basting until evenly browned. Put the skillet and meat in a (200°C) oven for 5-10 minutes. Remove the meat and rest in a warm place for 15 minutes. Gently heat 225g of pickles with the wine or port. Serve hot with the meat and garnish with fresh rosemary.
 Serves 4-6.

KUMARA OR POTATO CAKE TO SERVE WITH VENISON
2 large onions, chopped
4 tbsp olive oil
240g fresh tomatoes, peeled and cut in pieces
1 cup dry white wine

salt and pepper
900g potatoes or kumara in their skins
 Fry the onion in oil on a low heat until soft but hardly coloured, stirring often. Add the tomatoes and wine, and simmer for 30 minutes or until reduced to a thick sauce. Meanwhile, boil the vegetables until soft, then peel, mash and add gradually to the sauce, letting each spoonful become absorbed, until it has a firm, slightly moist texture. Serve hot shaped into a cake.
 Serves 8.

AUNTIE MARIE'S CHRISTMAS PUDDING
(makes 2 good 1.8kg puddings)
4 cups milk
250g butter
300g sugar
250g golden syrup (¾ of tin)
at least 850g mixed dried fruit, eg sultanas, raisins, cherries, lemon peel, dates, sliced dried apricots, currants, Christmas fruit mix (the type of fruit doesn't really matter)
2 heaped tsp baking soda
800g flour (wholemeal or plain or half each)
4 heaped tsp baking powder
 Once you are familiar with the recipe just relax about quantities and let the result be a surprise. It never fails! Put the milk, butter, sugar, syrup and fruit in a large pot, and simmer, stirring occasionally, until the fruit looks plump. Cool slightly before adding the baking soda (sometimes it appears curdled, but don't worry). Mix the flour and baking powder and add. Stir well and tip into 2 stainless steel bowls. (Jam, syrup or stewed fruit can be placed in the bottom of the bowls first to make a sauce when the pudding is tipped out.) Put the bowls into 2 pots of boiling water, ensuring that the water comes halfway up the bowls – no lids on the bowls, but tight lids on the pots. Boil for 2 hours – checking the water level – then remove, run a knife around to loosen the puddings and tip out. They can be frozen, and are good hot or cold.

CARAMEL SAUCE
400g butter
2 tbsp golden syrup
1 tsp vanilla essence
800g icing sugar
cream
 Melt the butter, golden syrup and essence and stir in the icing sugar. Alter the consistency with cream. It keeps well in the fridge.

Fleur Sullivan and her partner John Braine have run Clyde's award-winning Olivers Restaurant and Lodge for the past 15 years. Olivers, in true French provincial style, grows its own herbs, produces its own honey, and preserves summer bounty to enrich winter menus. Fleur's contribution to the tourist hospitality industry has been recognised with a number of awards, including a special Award for Enterprise in Tourism, 1992.

Auntie Marie's Christmas pudding with caramel sauce.

22

Bon appetit!

THE FAME of the Tipsy Tart made at Olivers Restaurant in Clyde has spread as far as the United States.

Restaurateur Fleur Sullivan has received a request from Bon Appetit magazine in Los Angeles for the tart recipe to feature in its RSVP column.

Recipes requested by readers who dined out frequently and travelled widely brought variety and excitement to the magazine and gave national publicity to fine restaurants all over the world, editor William Garry said.

The request comes soon after Ms Sullivan's plum pudding recipe featured in a The Listener's winter food feature.

A 1993 *Listener* winter food special. My recipes were featured along with those of Lois Daish, Annabel Langbein, Sue Leckie, Gillian Painter and Richard Till. All the recipes were prepared by one chef in the Olivers kitchen.

I didn't know what was going on until one of the staff told me that the young guy sitting at one of the tables was Jason Gunn, the children's television presenter. Not only did Jason not drink with his meal, he put the clean wine glass from his table onto the table beside him so that the kids wouldn't see him with anything associated with alcohol.

At other times there would be members of the New Zealand cricket team or the All Blacks whom I didn't recognise until the staff told me who they were. Once I was at a restaurant in Auckland and Jules Topp introduced me to her table of 12 friends saying, 'Fleur owns the most famous restaurant in Clyde!' Loved it!

However, it was the international patrons who really made Olivers financially successful. They were the ones who read the articles in the airline magazines and filled in their visitors' entry cards saying they were coming to New Zealand to visit Olivers and eat rabbit, venison and pickled walnut pies, which was fast becoming our signature dish. Tourism New Zealand assessed the surveys and came to Clyde to check us out, because a restaurant had never previously before been listed as a destination.

'What have you gone and done *now*?' Hunched over my horse's neck on the downward slope of a steep hill with a cavalcade of 200 horse riders, a gold coach, wagons, carts, gigs and buggies thundering and rattling behind me, I could hear Jim Sullivan's voice in my head. I wondered, briefly, whether this time I really had fooled 99.9 per cent of the people.

It was November 1991, and I was riding in the first Otago Goldfields Cavalcade that followed the Dunstan Trail from Middlemarch to Clyde. The adventure grew from an idea that had been brewing in my mind for some time before I raised it at an Otago Goldfields Heritage Trust meeting in 1990. The meeting had been discussing the fact that we only had about $35 in the kitty and we were wondering how we could raise the money to carry on promoting the area's heritage. I said, 'Why don't we do a re-enactment of the horse riders coming across the old Dunstan Trail to the goldfields every year on the anniversary of the first Cobb & Co coach ride?'

The Otago Goldfields Cavalcade

TOP
John Hore Grenell
and me at Naseby.

ABOVE
Holding up a train.

LEFT
Chris Fowle and me just
coming out of a blizzard.

RABBIT, VENISON AND PICKLED WALNUT PIE

The rabbit, venison and pickled walnut pie is something I first made in Clyde. People still ask if I will make it for them, or they ask me for the recipe. I used to make my own pickled walnuts too, but in Clyde I formed a special arrangement with Ian Mair of Stonehouse — I'd give him the walnuts and he'd do all the work! Stonehouse also makes a blackberry pickle that goes really nicely with this dish.

Serves 8

Ingredients
For the stock
rabbit bones (from the
meat used in the filling)
1 onion, chopped
1 carrot, chopped
1 stick celery, chopped
4 cloves garlic, chopped
1 cup red wine
salt and freshly ground
black pepper

RABBIT, VENISON AND PICKLED WALNUT PIE CONTINUED

For the filling
1 large onion, chopped
2 cloves garlic, crushed
3 slices smoked pork belly
(or streaky bacon)
olive oil, for sautéing
750g diced rabbit meat
(saving the bones for the stock)
750g diced venison
2 tbsp flour
1 cup stock
1 tbsp seeded mustard
1 tbsp tomato purée
1 tbsp fresh thyme, chopped
2 tbsp fresh parsley, chopped
1 tbsp Worcestershire sauce
80g mushrooms, halved
12 pickled walnuts
salt and freshly ground
black pepper

For the case
250g puff or shortcrust pastry
1 egg yolk or milk

Method

Make the stock by roasting the rabbit bones and vegetables in the oven until they begin to caramelise. This should take about 30 minutes. Transfer to a pot with the red wine and just cover with water. Simmer for 1½ hours. Strain the liquid off, discard the solids and bring to the boil. Reduce the liquid to 1 cup by hard boiling. Season to taste.

To make the filling, sauté the onion, garlic and pork belly in a little olive oil. Add the rabbit and venison and brown. Stir in the flour until it disappears, then add the stock, mustard, tomato purée, herbs and Worcestershire sauce. Cover and simmer gently for 45 minutes.

Add the mushrooms and pickled walnuts, and season with salt and freshly ground black pepper.

Preheat the oven to 220°C.

What you bake the pie in is up to you. I suggest large muffin tins, but you could also use ramekins or small pudding bowls — or throw the whole lot into a large pie dish. Line your chosen container with rolled-out pastry, fill, cover, brush with egg yolk or milk and crimp the edges together. Make a hole in the top of the pie with a skewer and decorate with pastry leaves and pastry walnuts.

Bake the pie for 30 minutes.

I serve these pies with quince paste and seasonal vegetables.

I loved my Doc Marten shoes!

Everyone said we should give it a go; we thought we might get about 50 participants. Well, 200 riders registered that first year with 240 horses and all the coaches and carriages. It was a truly exhilarating event and has been held every year since, with up to 800 participants at times. I took part in all the cavalcades before I moved to Moeraki, both on horseback and in a heavy wagon. It's one of the best holidays I can imagine.

In the early days when the calvacade was held in November you'd be likely to get frostbite and suffer from hypothermia in those high-country passes; now it's held in February. The trail starts and finishes in different parts of the region every year to promote different towns throughout Otago. Cavalcaders travel on horseback, in wagons or on foot for about a week and people come from all over the world to take part. It's been a phenomenally successful way to revive Central Otago history as well as horsemanship and all the ancillary skills.

Throughout my time at Olivers I was involved in local politics and heritage activities. I was an elected councillor, first on the Vincent County Council from 1988 until 1992 and then on the Otago Regional Council from 1992 to 2001. At the same time, from 1990, I have been a patron and life member of the Otago Heritage Trust, which has done a lot of good work in promoting the history of the towns in the region so that visitors have something to see and do when they get there.

In the mid-1990s, as usual, my life was hectic. The business was ticking along well enough and I was always coming up with new ideas to complement it — producing walnut oil as a commercial venture was to be the next scheme. I was also attending regular regional council meetings. When I was diagnosed with colon cancer in 1996 I felt it was just another hurdle I had to jump.

The tumour was very small but vicious, and the cancer had reached my bloodstream. I would need chemotherapy every week for a year. I was in hospital for about three weeks, I think, and received more flowers than you would ever believe. The other patients and the hospital staff were amazed. I said, 'Well, I've paid

The arch near where I built
the new stone wall.

a lot of people a lot of money for a long time. I know I've got some friends as well!' Just about anyone I'd ever had any dealings with sent bouquets. I suppose it gave a lot of people a fright and they wanted me to know they were thinking of me. It meant a lot.

I was admitted to hospital within days of being diagnosed. When I went down to Dunedin hospital I took a supply of biscuits and gourmet cheeses and a selection of the finest Central Otago wines for my visitors. When the hospital staff prepped me they asked me how much wine I drank every day because the nurses had told them what they'd found in my baggage. I also brought all my paperwork, thinking, Right, I'll catch up on all my bookwork.

I had a cellphone and found a toilet in the corridor that was much bigger than the one in the ward. I would stand at the far end, away from the door so that people couldn't find me, and make my calls. When the doctors were looking for me the other patients would say, 'She's in her office.'

I'd been told that I had to rest and stop any activity that could cause stress while I was having the weekly chemo treatment, but after I returned home to Olivers it soon became obvious there was no chance of that. Nobody seemed to take any notice of the fact that I needed to rest; they kept coming to me with little problems they should have been able to be deal with. After the weekly chemo dose I'd be sleeping in my room and someone would come over to say the filter on the fridge was clogged or a food order hadn't arrived or they wanted to put in for their holidays over Christmas.

Touching my scar in the early hours one morning soon after I'd had the surgery, I knew that if I wanted to get well I had to let go of everything that was holding me back. I made the decision to give myself a break and sell the restaurant. It was just luck that I didn't have to go through the horror of putting Olivers on the market but that didn't make the decision any easier. The couple who bought it told me they were looking for a business to buy and I said to them, 'Well, I want to sell mine.'

He was a bank manager and she was a chef, which seemed like the perfect combination. I showed them the bookwork and they took it away to study for a while and finally made the decision to buy on 17 March 1997, St Patricks Day. It was quite simple really, except for the grieving.

WHEN I WAS A TEENAGER, I ONCE VISITED MOERAKI. I'D FANTASISE ABOUT LIVING IN THIS BEAUTIFUL LITTLE SETTLEMENT: I LOVED THE FISHING FLEET BOBBING IN THE HARBOUR, THE GROUPS OF SEALS, HECTOR'S DOLPHINS AND YELLOW-EYED PENGUINS, AND THE HOMES PERCHED ON THE HILLS.

7

A WHALE'S
BLESSING

There are two more tiny villages, called Kaik One and
Kaik Two, on Maori leasehold land on the eastern shore.
A lighthouse still stands on the headland while the
marae and a school, which has since become the offices
for Te Runanga o Moeraki, are inland from the harbour.

In the 1940s and '50s there would have been only about 50 permanent
residents in Moeraki; even in 2011 there are fewer than 80, although a
lot of the holiday houses are more upmarket these days.

Moeraki is about 30 kilometres south of Oamaru and less than an
hour's drive north of Dunedin. For years most people drove past the
narrow dirt road that led off the highway and over the railway track to
the harbour. Instead they turned off the highway about 5 kilometres
away, just south of the village of Hampden at the entrance to Koekohe
Beach, where those huge, round rocks, the Moeraki Boulders, have
been scattered across the beach for 60 million years.

I always thought I wouldn't get to live at Moeraki until I was
about 108 but when I sold Olivers and needed to go somewhere
quiet to recuperate from the cancer it was the obvious choice.
Besides, it allowed me to be much closer to my mother in Oamaru.

I bought a very plain rectangular breeze-block house on the
highest hill in Moeraki because it had the view I wanted to look at
if I was destined to die on my couch. I could see the expanse of the
Pacific with Koekohe Beach and the boulders in the foreground,
Moeraki Harbour to the right and the farmland and hills to the
west where, on a good day, I could see the Remarkables.

I thought, When friends come to see me on my deathbed they won't feel so sorry for me if I have a view like this.

There was no garden around the house when I first arrived so I made compost and planted herbs, which is one of the most peaceful and restorative things you can do for yourself. My belongings were in containers in Central so Mike Hood and his wife Di packed a panelvan and a trailer with the cedar table that I'd found up in the rafters in the pack house while I lived in Alex, a couple of chairs, a bed, my chandelier, a desk, a TV, the couch and a few other bits and pieces and brought it to the house in Moeraki. For the next six months I came and went as I pleased because I was also looking after houses and accommodation businesses for friends in Central so I could be on hand to attend the Otago Regional Council meetings.

When I first shifted into the house I'd wake up in the morning and look down to the little promontory with the bay on one side and the harbour on the other. The site had been a whaling station in the 1830s and '40s. In the 1870s a big iron wharf had been built there and it was now used by the Moeraki commercial fishing industry. There was a walk-in chiller where the fishermen put their catch ready to be trucked away, a concrete-block room where they stored the live crayfish and a flight of steps on the outside of this building that led to a little smoko room.

Whenever I looked at that little parcel of land I'd think, You'll be very sorry one day if you don't buy it. As it happened, it came up for sale after a while and I was the only one who put in a tender, even though I didn't have any specific plans for it right then.

I loved foraging for wild foods around Moeraki. In season I found all sorts of fungi to identify and experiment with: puffballs, ink caps and field mushrooms taste fantastic cooked in a bit of butter with chopped wild herbs. I found Maori potatoes and native spinach on the edge of the beaches, in the hedges and at the penguin colony below the lighthouse on the far side of the promontory. New Zealand spinach grew best out of the sand at Kaik One and Kaik Two, the two settlements of fishermen's cribs. Since then I've been growing it in my garden and today we use it as a garnish on the muttonbirds and in our spinach oil in the restaurant. We've also got lots of wild parsley and we make our own rewena bread with the potato starter.

You meet the best people when you're out looking for puha. Then I caught eels and Fay Te Maiharoa showed me how to smother them with pepper and hang them in a tree to dry in the fresh air. When I bought a domestic smoker I took some smoked cod heads to the marae and everyone was too kind to tell me I'd left the gills in.

Meanwhile I'd come to know a few of the local fishermen and was invited out on the fishing boats. Oh, the seafood! I'd look longingly at the fish heads, frames, wings and livers being thrown out to sea and think of the things I could make with all that fresh fish waste. I considered making fish stock commercially, or rose fertiliser, but the idea that I liked best was to set up a little caravan on the jetty and sell chowder, smoked fish and fresh rewena bread.

Shortly after I shifted to Moeraki, I visited my friend Vaila in Invercargill. We were both invited to a party at the home of some of her Maori friends. I remember sitting there, observing my surroundings and all the interactions between people and wondering whether I could have lived that life, as Vaila had. Then I saw this gorgeously handsome guy and I thought, What would have happened if I'd been married to him?

He sat down on the floor at my feet with his back to me and started playing his guitar. Then this lovely man picked up my foot and started nibbling my toes! He said, 'My God, this foot's white!' 'So's the rest of me,' I said. He laughed and went back to playing his guitar.

I thought about how I could attract his attention. There was a bowl of prawn dip on the coffee table beside me so I stuck my toe into it and offered it to him, which seemed to make my toes all the more attractive. His name was Paaka Westrupp. We laughed and talked that evening and when we met up for coffee a day or so later, just before I was due to return home, I said to him, 'You should bring some friends with you and come up and take a look around Moeraki sometime.' He replied, 'Oh, I'm coming with you now.'

After he'd lived with me in Moeraki for a while, I began to gain an understanding of what it meant to be Maori in a way I'd never understood before. Paaka had lived in Invercargill for quite a while. This was Ngai Tahu country and he was Ngati Porou; I don't know whether I should have known about the implications of living in another tribe's area but I'd say to him, 'Don't be silly. Come to

the marae with me.' But he wouldn't come. As I got to know him better, I gained an insight into what it was like to be Paaka; I really appreciated the chance I had to be with him, to understand his being Maori and how he lived his life. He was true to himself, fluent in his own language and proud of his culture.

Paaka was a seasonal worker at the freezing works down in Invercargill. He was quietly strong and had learnt when not to speak, a habit he'd developed to get along in a Pakeha world. After we came to know each other we decided our past was irrelevant because neither of us could ever have understood what the other's life had been like. He told me he had been a whangai — fostered by his grandparents and other older members of his whanau in Gisborne. There were 14 children living in the house. One day when I talked to Paaka about not eating so fast, he said, 'If you'd grown up with four kids eating off one plate, you'd eat fast too.'

He had been in a gang, done time in a boys' home and prison, and had the tattoos that go with all that. He didn't expect anything from life other than what was freely available. He could live on nothing and not be bothered by it. If he had two of anything he gave one away. He taught me how to make boil-up with pork bones, cabbage and kumara, and when we took long walks around Moeraki he taught me where to find the biggest mussels and the best puha. In turn he was amazed and proud when I showed him the spots to find watercress and koura.

With time, as he got to know and trust me, he said, 'If you can love me like I love you, I will love and protect you for the rest of your life.' I'd never had that before; to find that he'd decided that he would trust me absolutely was a wondrous thing. I felt he was the man I'd been looking for all my life. I have no doubt that if things had turned out differently Paaka and I would have spent a lot of time exploring this country, visiting his friends and whanau from Bluff to the far North.

Before Paaka arrived, I knew I wanted to go back into business in a small way. The idea of setting up a caravan on the jetty to serve fish soup had expanded to include a fish smoker. I'd heard about the Mapua Smokehouse café in Nelson and was keen to check it out. Paaka told me he had two uncles, Johnny and Rangi Westrupp, who were musicians and also worked on cockle beds in

Golden Bay, so he said, 'We'll go and see them.'

When we were getting close to Nelson he wanted to pull off the road to get something to eat and I said, 'No, we're not eating till we get to Mapua because we've got to eat at the smoked-fish place. We've got to have a look at everything on the menu.' He couldn't quite get the hang of this; when we sat down I said, 'You'll have this and we'll have that, we'll both have that and we'll share this and share that.' Paaka said, in front of the waiter, 'Oh, I can't eat that much, Bub. I can't eat that much.' I booted him under the table and, once the waiter had gone, said 'We're doing a reconnoitre here and we need to eat everything on the menu!' But he kept saying, 'I'm not that hungry, I'm not that hungry!' Even though that was the sole reason for going there, he still didn't get it and thought I was being incredibly extravagant.

I saw a lot that interested me at Mapua but I knew I wanted my smokehouse to be much more visible and much more earthy. I knew I wanted people to be able to see the smoking process, and the fish coming out on the racks.

By this stage Paaka and I knew we would have very little time together. He had been diagnosed with cancer of the oesophagus before we went to Nelson and as he became more and more ill he said to me, 'I won't die in the South Island, Bub.' He went back to his people in Gisborne, wanting some time alone with his whanau, and I joined him there about three weeks later.

They had made him comfortable on a mattress in the lounge and there were more mattresses all over the large lounge so everyone could sleep near Paaka. It was all so achingly sad. In the end he was little more than a skeleton; he couldn't eat so he used a straw to drink a thick fluid that the hospital had prescribed to give him nutrients and keep him hydrated. I would change his pyjamas and bedding and sponge-bath him but in the end his whanau arranged for him to be admitted to hospital. I said my goodbyes to him and flew back to the South Island so that he could be with his own people at the end. But a few hours after I was back in Moeraki I received a call from Paaka's brother Trevor Westrupp to say Paaka had died. It was 22 August 2000.

❖

MOERAKI

A drawing by my son Martin, which we
used on T-shirts, menu covers and cards.

Paaka had been really enthusiastic about my idea of setting
up the smoker and caravan on the promontory and had been
looking forward to working on it with me.

Knowing that I could use the chiller as the kitchen and the
other room as a smokehouse, I told myself I could make the little
loft upstairs into a romantic getaway where people could stay
overnight and wake up looking out to the harbour. I could leave
a basket of breakfast goodies for them. However, it soon became
obvious that listening to the rattling and banging of the
equipment being loaded onto the boats, the roaring of the diesel
engines and the men calling to one another across the harbour at
5 am when the boats were preparing to go to sea for a day's fishing
was not the most romantic way to wake up, so I shelved that idea.

Meanwhile Brendon knew where I could buy a catering caravan,
and in time I got a hawker's licence. The notion of putting a sign out
on the highway reading, 'Fish smoker open 3 o'clock today' appealed
to me. I told myself it didn't mean I was going back into business.
Not really. People would just drive in; it would be like those places
I'd seen in France by the side of the road that sell goat's cheese.

When I first started serving food from the caravan I'd said to my kids, 'Maybe the whales will come back in. That'll sell lots of cups of tea!' Martin said, 'No, they'll never come in because Moeraki was a whaling station and this is where they were slaughtered — and whales have long memories.'

I didn't do any advertising but the word soon spread that I was in Moeraki and people began to arrive in numbers. On one particularly busy day Frederico and Meegan Gianone from Etrusco, the Italian restaurant in Dunedin, were there and Meegan started clearing away the plates because we needed a waitress for the caravan! When we'd finished up for the day I stood on the bank above the rocks and called out to the ocean, 'I don't need any whales, thank you very much! You can bugger off!'

Then Jim Hickey mentioned my smoked-fish caravan on the TV One weather report one night, and Kim Hill interviewed me on her Radio New Zealand programme. Before long there were so many people coming that the Waitaki District Council said I needed to provide toilets, designated car parks and a commercial kitchen. They wouldn't let me put the sign on the highway, nor would they permit me to have tables and chairs on my land near the caravan, so people used to bring their own. Eventually it all got too complicated. I thought, It looks like I'll have to build a restaurant.

By this stage I already had in mind the kind of place I'd like to build near the jetty. It had to reflect the history and heritage of Moeraki as a fishing port and whaling station with a strong Maori population, and I knew a couple of artisan builders, Rudie and Mark, who could make it look like it had been there for a hundred years. I already had a collection of old doors and windows, a Victorian-era wooden staircase and a whole house-lot of Southland beech that Mike Hood and I had carted away from Balclutha shortly after I left Olivers.

Then I spotted an old farm shed at Maheno a few kilometres north of Moeraki. It had once stood on the wharf at Kakanui just south of Oamaru and had been transported by two horse teams to Maheno decades ago. The shed was now on a lean and was going to be pushed over and burnt but there was enough timber for the floors and ceilings of the building I wanted to put up, including all the joists and beams. There was also the bonus that it was

ABOVE

Fleurs Place being built while
I was running the caravan.
Note the bay window!

RIGHT

Wearing my Goldfields
Cavalcade T-shirt.

BELOW

First 'evening diners'.

sitting on Oamaru stone blocks, which would also be very useful for the landscaping.

The owner, Mr McCone, was an elderly man and, because I went to see him several times, he thought there were a lot of women wanting his shed. Each time I saw him I'd tell him who I was and we'd have a chat and eventually I'd ask if he'd talked to his sons and made up his mind about selling the shed to me. He'd say, 'No, no. It's well sought after. It's a valuable shed. This other lady wants it.' So in the end I said to him, 'How about I offer you $1000 more than that other lady and we'll shake on it now because I need to get started.' So we shook on it and the shed was mine.

I wish it had been as easy to arrange things with the Waitaki District Council. I was driving to their offices in Oamaru several times a week, a 66-kilometre round trip. It took nine months for the various council officers to process all the permits and to define the compliances I had to meet before I could start building the restaurant. It seemed to me that every time I did something that was required in order to comply with the regulations there would be something else they hadn't mentioned, but which needed to be done. It was not a happy relationship. After a particularly frustrating visit, on the drive back to Moeraki, I was wondering how I was ever going to get this off the ground. Then I heard my father's voice saying, 'Don't let those bastards beat you!' I turned around and went back to the council office and said, 'I'm not leaving till this gets sorted.' To this day I get sick of defending myself against the nudge-nudge-wink-wink comments of people who are convinced that I built Fleurs Place without permits and in contravention of the regulations. That is simply not true.

Over a period of about three years I had to fight my way through what seemed to be deliberate obstruction by the council. The town planner told my draughtsman to make the restaurant look like a house so I could sell it when I went broke. Then once I'd opened the restaurant I couldn't get a permit to allow my patrons to eat outside. It seems they were in danger of damaging the environment so I had to pay for a very expensive environmental impact report. I circulated a survey around Moeraki and found no one minded people eating outside the restaurant but then the town planner said the council might object because of the noise

Scraping mussels in the rain at the Sandfords container.
Fiona, the chef of the Aotearoa Scallops dish, is the grand-
daughter of a pioneer sea captain who settled in Moeraki.

levels. I said I'd ask the fishermen to be a bit quieter when they set
up to leave the harbour before dawn each day and we'd share the
noise level fee. Then they were concerned about the smell of the
fish smoker, so I pointed out that Moeraki was a fishing port and
smelt of fish all the time. Someone else was worried that the
chimney of the old coal range in the corner of the restaurant
might fall and injure diners. Then there was the matter of the
upstairs balcony protruding about 15 centimetres beyond its
allowable overhang and the presence of the Sandford's chiller
at the back door of the restaurant.

The council insisted on having the fishermans' chiller moved
to the other side of the harbour; it was only after I'd built the
restaurant that they realised the chiller was sitting on Department of
Conservation land. DoC had no problem with the original arrangement so it seemed downright malicious of the council to remove it,
disrupting the working lives of the fishermen, making their jobs that
much harder and depriving the tourists of the chance to see the fish
being unloaded at the restaurant door. And so it went on.

Building Fleurs Place

The barn from Maheno.

My good friend Maureen and
me on the jetty at Moeraki.

The staircase from the
Hudson Homestead,
Dunedin. The Hudsons are of
Cadbury, Fry & Hudson fame.

Kirston, Ruby and me having a
break from laying foundations.

Me with Maurice Williams,
Marilyn's husband; the
window came out and went
back in.

The only picture of the whale in the bay.

My battles with the Waitaki District Council were covered in the local and regional newspapers. They were also documented in extended features in *North & South* in October 2003 and *The Listener* in June 2004. The articles included comments from the senior council officers who evidently 'chuckled' at my so-called eccentricities and said they were only applying the rules that they had to impose on anyone wanting to establish a similar business. It certainly didn't seem that way to me and besides, the questions have to be asked: What are these regulations designed to achieve and who benefits from them?

Meanwhile, on a particularly busy day early in 2002, a few weeks after Fleurs Place opened for business, one of the fishermen, John Higgins, walked in and said, 'Fleur, you might just like to tell your customers that there's a whale in the bay.'

I couldn't believe it! I went out and there it was, just a few metres from the bank, cruising up and down between the jetty and the curve of the bay. I went back inside and told the boys in the kitchen to turn everything off; that they had to come out and look at the whale. Then I told the people sitting at the tables to come outside and we all stood along the bank as the whale went backwards and forwards, backwards and forwards. As I watched it there were tears running down my face. I wanted to take my clothes off and walk into the sea. I thought, Oh, whatever they do to me, whatever happens to this place from now on, so be it. It's meant to be and it's beyond my control. Because what can you do? What can you do when a whale gives you its blessing? It glided through the water for several minutes then gave a wriggle along the whole length of its body and a slight flick of its tail, and it went away.

Later my friend Koa Whitau told me that her father, Richard Whitau, one of the kaumatua from Moeraki, had gone in to the council and said, 'You leave that girl alone. The whale appears to very few people. It is the father of a kaumatua from Kaik One and very few people ever see it. She is meant to be here.'

Three generations of family

Flame and Zeb,
Martin's children.

Earlier times; Martin's
birthday at the Walrus and
Carpenter, Alexandra.

Martin, Zeb, Flame, me
and Martin's partner Kat at
an exhibition at Dunedin
Art Gallery.

ABOVE
Brendon's children, Connor and Ella.

RIGHT
Fleur and Ruby at Olivers.

BELOW
At my investiture: Kirston, Mary Hardie Boys, the governor-general Michael Hardie Boys, me, my mother and Ruby.

I'D BEEN
PLANNING TO CALL
MY NEW RESTAURANT
'THE WHALE'S WAKE'
OR SOMETHING
SIMILAR. BUT FOR AT
LEAST A YEAR, WHILE
I WAS BUILDING
THE RESTAURANT
AT MOERAKI, PEOPLE
WOULD ASK, 'WHEN'S
FLEUR'S PLACE GOING
TO BE READY?'
THE NAME STUCK.

8

KEEPING
IT SIMPLE

Broadcaster Kim Hill asked me why there was no apostrophe in the name and I tried to explain that I didn't have a sense of ownership. The restaurant is just as it is. She didn't sound convinced.

Some people describe it as a glorified fishing shack and I'm happy with that. I wanted Fleurs Place to be an authentic part of Moeraki's fishing port. It had to look as if it had been on that 300-square-metre parcel of land on the spit leading to the jetty for a hundred years. All the doors and sash windows, the exposed timber beams, ceilings and floors, the fittings and furniture have had a long life somewhere else and come with a story.

I found the hull of an old fishing boat and had the builders use it as a screen around one of the toilet doors. Christchurch artist Andy Ducker made the beautiful copper and green metal undersea sculpture at the top of the bar and the talented Kirston Sullivan painted the whale's tail on the high window. There's a facsimile of Captain Cook's map of New Zealand and an old copy of the Treaty of Waitangi hanging on the walls alongside the fishing gaffs, the whale harpoons, the traditional Maori feather cloak and the old black and white photographs of Moeraki in the early days.

The tables and chairs once furnished the tearooms at the Oamaru racecourse. The tables originally had Formica tops, which the builders Mark and Rudie turned upside down to present the plain old wood. We keep them scrubbed and they are beautifully time worn.

RIGHT

The bar sculpture
by Andy Ducker.

BELOW

Limestone blocks
and fishing nets
form part of the
landscaping.

The chairs tell their own story; we ask notable guests to sign them with fat felt pens. A random sample of the names include Sam Hunt, David McPhail, Jon Gadsby, Fat Freddy's Drop, Dave Dobbyn, Marc Ellis, Jules and Lynda Topp, Prince Pomare of Tahiti, Leanne Malcolm, Jim Mora, Sir Tim Wallis, Lady June Hillary, Winston Peters, Paul Mercurio, Rick Stein, Olly Ohlson, Jason Gunn, Taine Randell, Anton Oliver, Keri Hulme, Gwyneth Paltrow, Chris Martin, Pam Ayres, the B-52s, the Tamati brothers, Tim Shadbolt, Mahinarangi Tocker, Suzanne Prentice, Tami Neilson, Peta Mathias, Gary McCormick, Annabelle White, Annabel Langbein, The Warratahs, Barry Saunders and the Silver Ferns.

There are some patrons I wouldn't ask for an autograph. I know that if Ralph Hotere signed a chair someone would walk out with it claiming they had a Hotere original, and who could blame them?

Even before we opened the restaurant the chairs had a story. I asked a young European WWOOFer to clean them up for me and he was amazed when he saw the stencil on the underside of the seats that read 'Made in Estonia' because that's where he was from.

I don't have an office at the restaurant, just a table beside the bar at the entrance to the kitchen so I can keep an eye on what's going out to the tables. When we're particularly busy and the table is needed, I clear away my paperwork so that two people can sit there.

I had the setting and ambience under control but when I established Fleurs Place in a bay with the sea on three sides, a fisherman's wharf and a trolley going into the sea to bring the fish in every night, I never dreamed that I wouldn't be able to buy fish in directly from the Moeraki boats. But as it turned out I couldn't. I became a licensed fish receiver but I still had to find a fisherman in the bay to sell me the fish!

Moeraki is a day port, which means the boats go out about 30 kilometres into the open sea each morning and return in the late afternoon. A lot of the fish sold throughout New Zealand comes off the big trawlers that spend days out at sea with their daily catch packed in ice. Then it has to be transported to the markets where it's sold to fishmongers and restaurants, which means the fish has

The *Fleur* was sitting in the harbour
when I arrived in Moeraki. Note the
fleur-de-lis on the cabin.

been on ice for a long time before it's eaten. There's nothing wrong with it, it's very good fish, but there's nothing quite like eating a meal of fish that has been caught just a few hours earlier.

The local commercial fishermen have their own quota, which they sell to the seafood wholesalers Sanford, Talley's and Kai Tahu (Ngai Tahu). When I first opened the restaurant I asked the fishermen if they would sell me some, but most of them didn't want to do the paperwork. They wanted to get off their boats and finish up for the day and they thought I was a nuisance. There were a couple of guys selling me small quantities but I needed more.

I couldn't understand why I wasn't able to buy some of the Moeraki catch on the wharf. The way I saw it, the fishermen would sell it to Sanford, Sanford would have the fish in the truck, they'd do the paperwork and sell it to me before they left the village. But that wasn't going to happen. I spoke to a senior manager at one of the companies and he told me they sold 95 per cent of their fish overseas. The whole of New Zealand is 5 per cent of their market. And he said to me, 'Where do you think you are in that 5 per cent?' So the fish was taken off to the Timaru depot and I would have to send Brendon to follow it because I was determined to have fish off the Moeraki boats that had come in that day.

I'd get out of bed, look down at the harbour and think, What day is it? It's Sunday. Oh my God, the sun is shining and we're going to be so busy. How much fish have I got?

I was so mad one day that I rang one of the bosses at Sanford at six in the morning and said, 'You've taken all this fish away from Moeraki and it's been sitting in your yard since Friday and won't be processed until Monday. And I've got all these people coming and you've got all the fish in your trucks.' Actually, stronger words were used.

When the driver came during the week, he said, 'Well, it looks like you can have what you bloody want. Here's my docket book. The boss said if you buy your own scales we'll do the paperwork for you on the wharf.' That worked well until the really high-tech electronic scales were introduced and they wouldn't let me weigh fish on my $1800 scales. But in the meantime I'd bought my own quota.

The blue cod quota from Area Three was selling for $35,000

a tonne at the time. Fortunately I was able to come to an arrangement with two brothers, Gavin and Kerry Te Maiharoa, to get tarakihi, groper, ling, moki, sole, brill and gurnard — but not blue cod — from them.

Then a local guy said to me, 'There's a bloke down at Taieri Mouth who wants to sell a quota for a couple of tonnes of blue cod along with a boat.' He took me down to have a look but it appeared that I'd have to buy a boat with the blue cod quota. That would mean I'd then have to hire a fisherman with all the ancillary problems of motors and breakdowns and the diesel costs — it was a nightmare just thinking about it. But I had to have that quota.

The guy who was selling it was a bit of a rebel. He knew I was desperate so he charged me $50,000 a tonne and I paid it. Then, by some miracle, a man came along and wanted to buy a boat without the quota.

I get enormous satisfaction from having my own quota and it's great to be involved in the commercial fishing industry as a licensed fish receiver. It gives me a huge marketing angle. The people who come here to eat love watching the catch being delivered to the door and having the fishermen standing around the bar with a beer after a day out at sea. They also come especially to see the fish being filleted and smoked. We buy loads of manuka and sometimes freshly milled oak. I add bay leaves and wild fennel that we've gathered from around Moeraki. We sell hundreds of our smoked kaimoana platters. When we first opened, most of the fish we sold was blue cod, but now people are more adventurous and choose other fish: the kaimoana platter includes a selection of interesting things to try like conger eel, octopus and paddle crabs.

One of my greatest pleasures is watching the fishermen with their boats. I look at them coming across the ocean with the seagulls following them and they're way down low in the water so I know they've got lots of fish. They come around into the harbour and, when the tide's low and they can't get their boat up to the wharf, one will stand in the dinghy and his mate in the back of the boat hands down the tubs full of fish. The one in the dinghy starts the outboard motor and he comes across the water to the trolley and cradle running on rails into the sea. He manoeuvres the

dinghy onto the trolley and we winch them up to the back door
of the restaurant. People just love watching all that, especially
children. Then we weigh the fish and do the paperwork.

Being a fisherman is very, very hard work and it's heartbreaking
to see how much equipment gets ripped or broken. The fishermen
aren't hard on their gear but it's just what happens. On the rough
days when they can't get out, they're all down there looking at
their boats, making sure they are secure. When it's particularly
bad weather with huge gales they have to take the boats out to sea
to ride out the storm; they can't afford to have them coming off
their moorings and crashing into one another in the bay.

With all this in my life, I think I'm the luckiest woman alive.
To have this ocean- and paddock-to-plate existence with crowds
of interesting people coming in to enjoy our naturally good food.
We are probably more fortunate than a lot of restaurants because

Fleurs Place is a destination. People purposely come here; they tell us where they've come from and how they came to hear about us, and we take the time to talk to them. I suspect a lot of restaurants don't have as much interaction with their patrons as we do.

After the 22 February 2011 earthquake in Christchurch we were run off our feet for weeks with people wanting to get out of the city and go somewhere calm and beautiful. One couple arrived the day after the quake. They walked in, hugged me and said they had lost everything but the clothes they were standing in but fortunately they had their wallets and credit cards. They had taken the first available flight out of Christchurch to Dunedin, bought some new clothes, rented a car and come to Moeraki because this was where they wanted to be to get over the shock. I put them in a quiet corner upstairs, fetched them a drink and they stayed there all evening.

And don't let anyone tell you Kiwis are undemonstrative. A lot of hugging goes on here. It's often the case that if people don't hug you when they walk in, they're hugging you when they leave. And of course they're not all New Zealanders, they're from all over Europe, the States and often the most obscure and fascinating places. I was very touched when people started telling me that Fleurs Place was on their bucket list. It might have taken them three years to get here but they'd read about it and they were determined to come. Or there are people who've been here only once, years ago, and they tell me they've been thinking about the fish soup all the way down from Taihape.

We have established a truly regional restaurant. We have to be consistent because people come with specific expectations, so they are disappointed if the meal isn't the way they've enjoyed it before or the same as a word of mouth recommendation. They come for a memory and the taste of fresh fish, for the setting and the ambience. And I suppose I have to acknowledge that making people feel welcome and special is something that I was born into.

There are people who walk through the door with the expectation that they will meet Fleur. I love talking to everyone when they're seated and while I'm signing a book or a person's serviette or a magazine article. On the other hand, people know I've been around for 45 years in one restaurant or another and some of them assume I've put my feet up. They'll say, 'Oh, we didn't expect to find you

here.' And I'll say, 'Well, why would I stay home when I can have all this?' But being there is all important. I know how much I hate having my plate taken from me before I've finished!

There was a man who walked in recently with nine different varieties of potato wrapped up in serviettes labelled with the name of each one. They were his return koha because I had given him some heritage seed potatoes last time he was here. I don't know his name or where he comes from in the North Island but we talked potatoes, he had a meal and off he went again saying he'd see me in another couple of years.

Then there was the man from MAF who was here recently. He reminded me that we last met when he interviewed me while I was in bed with cancer in Clyde and he'd had to talk to me about some illegal rabbit meat in the fridge at Olivers. I remembered him as a nice man with a lovely face and a job he had to do. The Ministry of Ag and Fish (MAF) can search your restaurant fridges at any time, and when he saw that the quantities of my special pie mix didn't tally with the amount of rabbit I'd bought, he'd had to come over to my bedroom to see my paperwork.

At that time, as I've said before, the rabbits used in commercial operations had to be imported from China for $28 a kilo, bones and all. They looked like whitebait. They were horrible things and I had to buy them to make my best-known dish: the rabbit, venison and pickled walnut pie. This was before the rabbit calicivirus was illegally liberated from a blender in Tarras, and we had lovely retired rabbiters who'd shoot the rabbits fed on wild thyme and briar rosehips in the hills around Clyde and prepare them perfectly for $5 a pair. They'd present them like pearls with pure white baking paper between each one, as if they were giving you a beautiful gift. To be honest, I seldom used those Chinese rabbits. I had to buy them so that I had orders and receipts to show MAF where I got my rabbit meat from but I hated using it in my beautiful pie that brought tourists to New Zealand.

So I said to him, 'Please don't throw it away! Please take it home and give it to your friends. Please, I can't bear it!' The pie filling takes hours of prep: roasting the bones, picking and pickling all those walnuts, marinating the meat and making the beautiful sauce. But two fish tubs of it were chucked into the

Rick Stein at Moeraki. My pet Canadian
goose, hand-fed on puha, is in the
background.

mighty Molyneux (that's what the old-timers call the Clutha
River). The eels probably ate it. But anyway, we now had a good
laugh and a hug. I said, 'Who do you work for now?' He's still
working for MAF.

It's an honour to have a busy restaurant with repeat business
and lovely people who've obviously driven a long way. Quite a
few of them are on fixed incomes and I never fail to appreciate
that they're spending money that might otherwise pay for a week's
groceries. There are New Zealand artists, like Keri Hulme, who
wrote *The Bone People* at Kaik One; when she's in the area she
comes here. And to serve Ralph Hotere some beautiful seafood
is a joy. It makes his whole face light up.

When the English restaurateur and TV food-show host Rick
Stein walked in, he said, 'Oh, my producer would die for the
visuals in the place.' I had to say to him, 'There's been a lot of

rough weather so the boats haven't been out for four days.'
When he wrote about his visit later, he said that was exactly what
he needed to be told. He didn't mind at all because he knew what
it meant for a fish restaurant to be dependant on the weather.

And I knew exactly how he felt about trying the food. He didn't
want to sit and have a meal off the menu, he just wanted to taste
everything, so I bought him small dishes of smoked fish from the
kaimoana platter, titi or muttonbird with native spinach and
puha, Gilbert's goose-liver parfait and Missie's bacon-wrapped
blue cod with cockles.

He told me that when a newspaper had offered to send him to
a restaurant anywhere in the world to have lunch and write about
it, he had chosen Fleurs Place. In the article he wrote later he said
that whenever he was in the company of other foodies and they
talked about fish, Fleurs Place was always mentioned.

It was a pleasure to meet him and people often ask, 'What was
he like? Was he as nice as he is on TV?' Of course he was. He's just a
thoroughly lovely, unpretentious man. Before he left, while we were
walking around outside the restaurant to take in the setting he said,
'I wish I could go further down the coast in Cornwall and start again
and keep it simple.' In a subsequent article a journalist asked,
'What did you learn from Fleur?' and he said, 'To keep it simple.'

Another memorable occasion was when we had a call from a
limo driver on a wet Sunday while we were very busy and the
kitchen was struggling to get the meals out. The windows were
steamed up, there were children playing about, we were waiting
for the boat to come in and he wanted to know if we had room for
a couple of Americans. I suggested he try to book them into Bell
Pepper Blues or Corstorphine House in Dunedin but he told me
they wanted to come to Fleurs Place. I said we'd probably be able
to find room for them.

When these two young people came in I didn't take too much
notice of the guy but the girl had this lovely aura about her. I said,
'Oh my God, you're a beautiful girl.' She quickly stepped back so I
put my arm around her and said, 'Don't worry, it's OK.' I didn't want
to frighten her. I said, 'It's OK, but you *are* a very beautiful girl', and
then as I was leading them upstairs I looked at her again and said,
'Oh, are you maybe Gwyneth Paltrow or someone?' She just smiled

SEAWATER CHEESE

Is it worth the trouble to make such a small amount of this recipe — it's not expensive and very delicious so triple the recipe and give some to your neighbour. I've never used the 'home-made' seawater, so collect a bucketful of seawater from a clean part of the ocean and you'll be really satisfied with the result. You can add chives, thin slices of pepper or parsley as it chills. Serve with potted smoked eel, cod's liver pate and rewana bread.

Makes approximately ⅔ cup

Ingredients
3 cups seawater
(or plain water with 25g salt dissolved in it)
3 cups full cream milk

Method
Heat seawater and milk in a large saucepan. As the liquid begins to boil, it will separate and curds will form. Remove from heat at once and pour through a cheesecloth-lined sieve to capture the curds.

Hold the sieve in a bucket filled with ice-cold water to stop the curdling process. Tie the corners of the cloth together and hang for about 30 minutes to strain off any excess liquid.

You will then have about ⅔ cup of lovely sweet, soft cheese. Serve with crusty bread on an antipasto platter or cheese board.

quietly and said, 'Yes, I am.' I said, 'Oh, that's fine.' And up we went.

It was only later when every magazine in the universe started ringing up to find out what they'd eaten, what they were wearing and what they'd said to anyone that I realised what a big deal it had been to have had Gwyneth Paltrow and Chris Martin in the restaurant. As far as I was concerned, the fact that she was known to eat healthy organic food and had chosen to come here was a huge recognition of our naturally good food.

At the time there were three or four teenagers in Moeraki who happened to be home from boarding school. Somehow the word got out that Chris Martin from Coldplay was at Fleurs. They all turned up at the door saying, 'Fleur, can I carry a plate up? Can I clear the table? Can I bring them some water?' I said, 'Well, you can't go to their table but you can carry something to another table so you can have a look.' The table is now known as Gwen's table.

When their wedding was announced, people were saying, 'Did you see Gwyneth's getting married?' as if she was a close personal friend. I'd say, 'Yes, I'm adding the extensions to the restaurant.' There were even some people who were surprised that I hadn't been invited to the celebrations.

Managing the staff is a major part of running any restaurant. Other than the executive chefs, for the most part I employ a group of young people who have trained at the polytechs. They've usually worked in a tavern or two but never in a restaurant like this. I have to train them to work well together, understand the special nature of this place and to do exactly what I tell them.

I don't often throw a wobbly in the kitchen but I do remember one time when the owners of Mantells restaurant in Auckland booked a table for eight and I wanted them to have the very best of what we have to offer. A load of fish had come up in the dinghy an hour before they arrived so I took the fish into the kitchen and said, 'This is for the Mantells' table.' I told the staff that these were very important patrons and that one of their family, my friend Koa Mantell, lives in Moeraki.

Later, as I was taking the plates to the table, I realised it wasn't the right fish. There is something about blue cod straight out of the sea, and this wasn't it. Some of the plates had gone out and I said to the kitchen staff, 'Is this the fish I told you to use?' Somebody looked up and said, 'Oh, no, it's not.' I said, 'Right, stop.' I went out to the table and said, 'Give me that food back.' And of course some of them had started eating. I said, 'This is not the fish I wanted you to have.' And they looked at me and they sort of clutched their plates and said, 'It's lovely, it's lovely, we want it.' And I said, 'No! It's not what I wanted you to have. Give me your plates back!'

I took the plates into the kitchen but they weren't taking any notice of me because we were so busy, so I got a $30 box of lettuce off the bench and jumped up and down on it and they all stopped. I said, 'Cook the meals again with the fish I asked you to use.'

At the end of that day the young chef who was in charge in the kitchen was pretty upset about it. I went outside and sat with him in a dinghy and talked to him about why I wanted things done the way I wanted, that it wasn't just anywhere he was working, that it wouldn't have made it as a restaurant if it was. I told him I didn't make the restaurant for him, I made it for Fleur. When he got his own restaurant he could do whatever he wanted, but in the meantime, this was my restaurant and this was how he'd do it. He had to forget all the tricks he'd learnt in other places and do it my way.

I used to serve breakfasts in the restaurant, which meant everyone in the kitchen had to be a little bit smarter and faster in the morning, given that we have a small kitchen and we have to prepare a lot of fresh produce each morning, including the soup. Often there'd be a few staff who were in no mood to cook breakfast for anyone apart from themselves, depending on what they'd done the night before. I'd look in the sink and see the evidence of their own scrambled eggs and sausages, but as soon as I wanted breakfast for the customers, they'd grumble because they still hadn't had their coffee.

One morning I'd had enough of the clanging and banging and crashing in the kitchen in response to a breakfast order. I went in and I said, 'Fleurs as we know it is over. I'll be closing two days a week. And there'll be no more breakfasts.' One of the staff said, 'What does that mean?' And I replied, 'Don't order any more sausages, because it's over.' I absolutely hated doing that but it simply had become too hard to keep repeating myself day after

CULLEN SKINK SOUP

Traditionally made with smoked haddock, Cullen skink originated in the village of Cullen on the north-east coast of Scotland. The first day we had this on the menu, I was explaining the soup to a table of five who cut me short by saying, 'Och, we come from Cullen'!
Serves 4–6

Ingredients
40g butter
1 leek, trimmed and roughly chopped
4 cups fish stock
2 small waxy potatoes,
peeled and cut into 2 cm cubes
1 bay leaf
300g smoked firm-fleshed fish,
bones removed and flaked into pieces
¼ cup cream
1 tbsp parsley, chopped
freshly ground black pepper
4–6 free-range eggs

Method
Melt butter in large saucepan over a medium heat. Add leek, cover and cook gently for 10 minutes or until soft. Add stock, potatoes, bay leaf and smoked fish. Simmer gently for 10 minutes or until vegetables are tender. Stir in cream and parsley and season with pepper.

Poach an egg for each person, leaving yolk soft. Ladle soup in each serving bowl and place a warm egg on top. Serve.

day and year after year.

Just as at Dunstan House and Olivers, the food style at Fleurs
Place is based on fresh local produce served with the minimum
of interference with its natural texture and flavour. We serve
beautiful sauces, herbs, spices and simple garnishes that give the
dishes just the right twist. The fresh vegetables are steamed and
have a firm bite; the salads include edible greens and flowers
foraged from the countryside around the restaurant. Some front
of house staff and chefs take a basket when they walk to work
so they can pick wild parsley, fennel and spinach as well as
nasturtiums, blue borage and passionfruit flowers.

The taste and presentation of most of our dishes are deceptively
simple. A lot of talent, expertise and restraint go into creating them.
So I smile a bit if I hear people saying, after they've eaten here,
'I could cook that! Why am I paying $30 for a bit of fish and some
undercooked veges on a plate?'

These people are not seeing the big picture, which is that the
food is meant to be natural and that the ambience, the location,
the furniture — everything right down to the mismatched cutlery
and crockery — is designed to give them a sense of conviviality,
generosity and warmth.

Inspiration for the dishes that become our bestsellers can strike
at any time. One morning I went into the kitchen to find that Errol,
one of the chefs, had created a new fish pie. He had the dishes lined
up, ready to go in the oven. I said, 'Errol, you can't make a new
dish like that. We have to taste it, we have to look at it, we have to
understand what's in it and why you put it in.' So we all inspected
this new dish before he cooked it.

When it came out of the oven it had crumpled-up filo pastry on
top; I was terrified! Filo pastry? But people love it. They say, 'That's
the best fish pie that I've ever tasted!' I thought, My God! This
boy's made the best fish pie in the world with no fuss. That was
a good day.

On another day, I woke up thinking we needed another new dish
on the menu. Missie Hollows had created the bacon-wrapped blue
cod with cockles, which is our all-time bestseller. Simon Peacock's

best creation was the shellfish hotpot with fresh fish, mussels, cockles and scallops, and Maori potatoes and Maori spinach. But I wanted to create a hapuka dish. Whenever I get a tub or two of this magnificent fish, I want to sell it straight away in peak condition.

Imagining the texture and flavours in my mouth, I thought, Because the hapuka is such a thick fillet, we can make a carpetbag and stuff it with mussels. I asked the staff whether we should use fresh steamed mussels or smoked mussels and everyone voted for smoked. Chef Meg suggested putting a wee bit of anchovy in with the butter and the mussels on the top. It's a winner when we have hapuka!

My suppliers are nearly all within an hour's drive of Moeraki. I get fabulous shellfish from Roger Belton of Southern Clams, who harvests from Blueskin Bay on the Otago Peninsula. He supplies us with fresh, chilled, live queen scallops and the molluscs that have become known as littleneck clams — in Moeraki we still call them cockles.

We get a lot of produce from people who have stalls at the Otago Farmers' Market in Dunedin. Chris Larcombe and Viviene Scott own Kakanui Produce; as well as running their stall at the market they supply us with beautiful organic tomatoes and greens. Susan Randell runs Mean Greens and brings us watercress, rocket, mizuna, mesclun and interesting lettuces from her glasshouses in Oamaru. The lovely Alison MacTavish lives here in Moeraki and has gone into Maori potatoes in a big way. There are several different varieties and we use them in a lot of dishes. She also brings us all sorts of green things like Florence fennel, cavolo nero, Chinese brassicas and miner's purslane, which most people think of as an invasive weed but it tastes delicious and has a high nutritional value. I'd love to have the garden Alison keeps if only I had time, but she says she envies what she calls my 'mind-map' of all the wild apple trees, wild fennel and clumps of cress that grow around Moeraki. We also get a lot of our vegetables from Reggie Joe, a Chinese market gardener at Totara on the outskirts of Oamaru. Our asparagus comes from Rod Phillips near Palmerston and our cheeses come from Bob, Sue and Simon Berry's international award-winning Whitestone Cheese factory in Oamaru. We get all our free-range eggs from a lovely man at Shag

Point just a few kilometres away but I've now been told that soon I've got to buy them from a certified free-range poultry farmer.

There are any number of elements that contribute to creating the right atmosphere in a restaurant. Besides the setting, the aesthetics, the food and the people, I've always recognised the value of live ambient music. It has to be the right music played at just the right volume and that's why Mike Hood is here. Just as he was the resident musician at Olivers for all those years, Mike has been playing regularly at Fleurs Place since 2002.

We've been good mates who have helped each other through some pretty rough times for nearly 30 years.

Living in Moeraki, I've noticed how many men are hunter-gatherers in their spare time. Quite a lot of them are of an age but there are young guys doing it as well. I didn't notice it so much in Clyde, even though some locals provided me with rabbits and wild game.

In the evenings when they come to Fleurs Place for a drink I'll put down a platter of titbits made up from the leftovers of the day. One of the most frequent topics of conversation is how they make their rabbit pie or jugged hare, or how they use the cod's heads and livers from their fishing trips. Big Ev from Hampden comes in a lot. He's a really tall, heavy-set bloke, and he was telling us recently about the way he makes his chutneys and pickles. Gav Te Maiharoa, who gets my fish for me, has sausages made by the butcher in town using meat from his own animals and ones he's hunted.

A while ago I had a batch of venison sausages made by my usual butcher and for some reason they didn't turn out as I wanted. They tasted fine but the texture was wrong and I didn't want to serve them in the restaurant so I offered them to Martin Finney, who runs a charter boat. I thought his clients might like them when they were out on the water but I couldn't give them away! Martin said he was very particular about his own sausage recipe which he has made by the butcher in Palmerston.

A lot of the men around here also keep vegetable gardens and hens, which is something I'd recommend for everyone who has

Dougal McDougall filleting fish
outside Fleurs Place.

even a small backyard.

I've kept hens since the early days on the West Coast, and of course I grew up with them. I had them for a while when we were living in the A-frame in Queenstown but the neighbours objected to the roosters crowing and my lease said I wasn't allowed pets so I was stymied there.

I had beautiful little white Chinese silkie bantams running around on the lawn at Olivers and when I moved to Moeraki I had a fair number of hens and roosters. The neighbours, who stay here about four times a year, made a fuss about them and the Waitaki District Council got involved so in the end I had to have the poultry slaughtered. A lot of people came to help me. Martin Finney came up and shot some of them in the trees and Brendon snared others. Each day as more were killed, Mary Whitau, one of my friends from Moeraki, and I plucked them at the back of the restaurant. One day a man going past said, 'Oh, do you mind if I take a photo of you two plucking muttonbirds?' And I said to Mary, 'If it was me, a Pakeha, sitting here by myself, I'd be plucking a hen, but because you are Maori, they think we're plucking muttonbirds!' We had lots of laughs about it.

Gilbert Prevost, the French chef from Olivers days who had come back to work with me, taught me how to use the giblets and the whole flock made beautiful staff meals for quite some time.

We saved all the feathers and Mary made a big cloak — the korowai — that now hangs on the wall in the restaurant. She wove in some beautifully coloured pukeko feathers that I'd found on the side of the road and in the bushes on my regular foraging trips. People have been married in that korowai and this has started a whole new interest for Mary. She's now making and selling feather bags and cloaks.

When I stood up to be inducted into the New Zealand Restaurant Hall of Fame in 2007, Mary and our friend Koa Mantell draped me in a new cloak that Mary had made. It made me cry.

But the whole chicken-and-egg cycle has begun again because after the slaughter I was in the bathroom one day and heard 'cheep cheep cheep'. One little hen had escaped and came to the window to show me her chicks.

The idyllic life you often find when you first arrive in a small, isolated community where families have lived together for generations has its dark side. The same community often harbours people with a belligerent resistance to newcomers and a strong homophobic bent. I found this to be true in Clyde and it is also a fact of life in Moeraki.

The hospitality industry tends to attract a number of people who don't necessarily fit into the mainstream, so Fleurs Place is not just about sourcing fresh local food and serving it to charming patrons while interacting with colourful local characters. It's also about keeping some 17 staff housed, concentrating on their work and out of trouble.

There's not a lot to do in Moeraki in the evening so they will sit around in one or other of the nine staff houses I provide playing cards and drinking, or they will go out for a few hours to the tavern in the Moeraki village or at Hampden, less than 10 minutes' drive away. And in these places it's not at all uncommon for them to have to cope with some fairly unpleasant behaviour from a number of the locals, who will taunt and insult them, saying 'You'd be a poof, a shirt-lifter, a turd-pusher working for her, wouldn't you?'

Some of my staff have a few affectations, with their scarves and their shoulder bags, and I say to them, 'Don't pull up at the pub, tossing your scarf while you walk in! Remember where you are!' Over the years I've had to say to them, 'Some of those guys in the pub, if they took offence, would burn your house down — my house, actually — or burn your car. They will act like redneck, bigoted hillbillies.'

In the time I've been in Moeraki I've said, 'You've got children growing up. What sort of example are you setting them with your bigoted, preconceived ideas?' But they tell me they would shift their kids from the school if they thought one of the teachers was gay. They're a little bit more open-minded about lesbians because they think if they got them out on a boat all they'd need would be a jolly good rogering in the wheelhouse and they'd change their mind.

So when a boy comes to work here sporting an earring and

My son Martin drew this
for our wine list cover.

frosting in his hair he's likely to get a hard time from a few of the locals. Recently a staff member, who has been here about three years, was carrying five coffees and one of the local guys gave him a nudge and knocked them out of his hand. Someone else took a car key and scratched the word 'fag' across his car bonnet. He didn't care, he just left it there and drove around the town with it.

With some incidents I think I can talk to the offenders myself. I know that they are bigoted and I know they're not going to change but I try to make them understand that it's not acceptable. No staff, no restaurant. Simple really.

I wake up every morning eager to go to work in this beautiful place. My first thoughts are: What's the weather like? How much fish have I got? Are the boats out? What day is it? Some days are busier than others and if it's the weekend and the weather's good there's likely to be a full house.

We have a responsibility at Fleurs Place because we have been recommended to people all over the world and throughout New Zealand. We need the boats to come in with the fish and to have happy customers — and then all's well in the world.

But there are still too many opportunities to embrace. When I was at Dunstan House I wanted an art gallery and antiques shop on site. Olivers restaurant became a lodge with artisan shopkeepers operating out of the courtyard and my interest in history and heritage took care of any spare time I might have had. So instead of sitting back, I decided to open another restaurant.

ALL HOOKS, TRUCKS &c
in use in the store
TO BE PUT BACK HERE

Desserts 11·50

♡ Chai scented
creme brulée

♡ Poached pear in
spiced red wine w̄
Meringue

♡ Rice pudding w̄
confit apple

♡ Seasonal fruit Crumble
w̄ runny cream.

♡ Central Otago Apricot
bread & butter
pudding

$-42

$-35 $-4 $-34

THREE HUNDRED
AND FIFTY PEOPLE
SIT ELBOW TO
ELBOW ON CHURCH
PEWS AND BENCHES
AT EITHER SIDE OF
A SERIES OF LONG
WOODEN TABLES
SET WITH VINTAGE
CUTLERY AND
CROCKERY,
COMMUNAL BUTTER
DISHES AND JUGS.

9

THE LOAN & MERC

Breads and cheeses, seasonal fruit, vegetables and bunches of herbs are displayed on enormous sideboards around the walls. The huge wood-fuelled firebox that heats the cavernous room looks like a Heath Robinson–steampunk collaboration.

In the evening we serve a carvery with haunches of rare roast beef, lamb, pork and venison served with vegetables, salads, sauces, mustards and relishes, followed by a choice of three or four traditional desserts. During the day we offer an elaborate ploughman's lunch with about 40 items to choose from. We always have a few à la carte dishes too, like colonial goose and my rabbit, venison and pickled walnut pie.

The restaurant's front room is a bar where we serve regional wines, craft and boutique beers, good whisky and simple $10 bar meals like rare-beef open sandwiches and executive chef Gilbert Prevost's wonderful house-made sausages.

I've furnished the restaurant with antiques and had the long wooden tables made from the heavy timber leftover from the shed I demolished to build Fleurs Place. The recycled timber we used to build the new kitchen came from the floor of the Balclutha cricket club and the sprig marks are still in it. I'd had it in storage for about 12 years.

✣

Gilbert Prevost at the carvery at the Loan & Merc.

LOAN & MERC HERB AND GARLIC PORK SAUSAGES

It's great to watch the deft movements of Gilbert, Kwan and Tony producing these beautiful house-made sausages.

Makes as many as you wish depending on their size

Ingredients

1kg pork collar or shoulder meat
300g pork back fat
15g salt
10g white pepper
20g dried herb mix
bunch fresh thyme, chopped
bunch fresh parsley, chopped
30g garlic, freshly chopped
1 litre iced water
2 metres sausage skins

Method

Chill the pork and back fat to close to freezing temperature, and coarsely mince. Add the seasonings and iced water, and mix thoroughly. Put the mixture through the sausage maker.

I had fantasised about creating a restaurant like the Loan & Merc in Oamaru for decades. Even when I was in Clyde I used to think how wonderful it would be to do what I'd done there in the old part of Oamaru. It was only a brief fancy because at that time, the 40-odd buildings in what is now Oamaru's Historic Precinct were derelict; the area didn't really come to life until the mid-1990s.

In 1882 the New Zealand Loan & Mercantile Building at the south-eastern edge of the original commercial and business district was a grain store housing 100,000 bags of wheat. It now has New Zealand Historic Places Trust Category I status, which is given to buildings of 'special or outstanding historical or cultural heritage significance'. Along with another 14 buildings in the precinct, it's owned by the Oamaru Whitestone Civic Trust.

A friend on the trust board contacted me in the middle of 2010 and suggested I take a look inside the building to see what possibilities it might suggest. It didn't *suggest* anything. It *insisted* that it become a Victorian banqueting hall. By the time I walked out I had already furnished it in my mind and set the menu. It seemed that it was meant to be — just look at how many copper jam pans and how much linen, fiddle and thread cutlery, old crockery and demolition timber I've got!

The building is three storeys high and I've leased the ground floor — a bit more than 1300 square metres — it's bigger than a quarter-acre section. It has Oamaru stone throughout, and beautiful arched windows and bare wooden floors. Because the grain was stored on all three storeys, the space is divided by sturdy support columns made from Australian hardwood and Port Chalmers blue stone. Three big elevators used to carry bags of grain from one floor to the next; the trust has restored one of these to working order.

I began talking seriously to the people at the Civic Trust after I'd looked through the building. We were hoping to have the restaurant up and running in time for the Victorian Fête, held in the historic precinct in the third week of November every year, but that turned out to be a bit too ambitious for 2010. We didn't really get started until December.

I have a good working relationship with the trust. They put in the plumbing, drainage and switchboard and built the shell of a

Loan & Mercantile, established in 1882.

HAPUKA ON ROASTED CAPSICUM WITH SMOKED MUSSELS

Chef Gilbert Prevost's version of our hapuka
dish at the Loan & Mercantile in Oamaru.
Serves 4

Ingredients

1 red capsicum
1 green capsicum
extra virgin olive oil
½ onion, sliced
3 cloves garlic, chopped
2 star anise
2 cloves
freshly ground black pepper
1 sprig fresh thyme
4 hapuka fillets (about 180g each)
16 smoked mussels
salt
plain flour, for dusting
splash of dry white wine
a little fish stock (made with fish trimmings)
fresh garden herbs (such as thyme, parsley
and chervil), chopped, for garnish

HAPUKA ON ROASTED CAPSICUM WITH SMOKED MUSSELS CONTINUED

Method

Roast the red and green capsicums in a hot oven, then peel and slice. In a heavy-bottomed pan combine a little oil, the roasted and sliced capsicums, onion, garlic, star anise, cloves, black pepper and thyme. Cook until the mixture reaches the consistency of jam then put aside in a dish that can also be used later as the serving dish.

Make an incision in the fish fillets and fill with four mussels each. Season the fillets with salt then dust with flour. Pan fry until the fish has just cooked through. Set the fillets on the capsicum mixture then deglaze the frying pan with the wine. Pour over the fish stock. Cook for a further 15 minutes in the oven. Add a sprinkle of chopped herbs, a drizzle of oil, and salt and pepper to taste.

new kitchen, which I furnished with appliances. Their members held working bees and cleaned up 120 years of grime and dust. And, thank God, the trustees handled most of the negotiations with the Waitaki District Council. I think some of the people on the committee who had never dealt with their local council over issues of compliance were given an insight into the difficulties of trying to get a business off the ground.

Phil Hope, who is trust chairman and a lawyer as well, worked with my builder to arrange the consents with the Waitaki District Council. They found it a frustrating experience, which was no surprise to me after my years of battles with some WDC employees.

The council's biggest concern was the fact that the previous tenants still had 144 barrels of single malt and blended whisky on the first floor above the space where we wanted to build the restaurant. Some people working for the council were very concerned about this, so they took months to process building consent applications and liquor licences.

They had decided that the barrels of whisky were a flammable, hazardous substance because they were in proximity to a gas-fired kitchen. Phil pointed out that science says they couldn't explode unless there were extreme temperatures of 400°C, but to work through all those issues seemed to involve eight or nine local and central government agencies and a lot of hysteria that took the best part of a year.

Of course I am always asked, 'Why? Why open another restaurant?' And I always answer, 'Because I can. And because it needs to be done.'

Once again, you have to look at the big picture. Just like the main street of Clyde, Oamaru's historic precinct needs to be preserved. Not just in terms of maintaining some lovely, empty buildings; it needs to be brought to life with people earning a living there. And that means a lot of people need a reason to go the precinct and spend money.

It's not as if I needed the headache of running a second restaurant. But ever since Noel Allen and I used to play there, pretending we'd just got off a sailing ship in the harbour and were exploring a ghost town, I've always loved the precinct. I want to make a contribution towards its future.

It's wonderful! It's an authentic Victorian business and commercial district with dozens of lavishly ornate limestone buildings on the edge of a pretty Victorian-era harbour with its wharves and jetties, and a breakwater where huge waves crash and explode in plumes of white foam. On the far side of the harbour, just 10 minutes' walk from the front door of the Loan & Merc, there's a collection of old red railway sheds where craftspeople have their workshops, and a managed colony of little blue penguins that brings something like 80,000 people to Oamaru every year. I want every single one of those people to come into the precinct to shop and eat.

There are more than 40 businesses and organisations working out of the buildings in Harbour and Tyne streets, the two best-developed areas in the precinct. Some of them have been there since the mid-1990s, like Willetts furniture makers, the beautiful old Criterion Hotel, Michael O'Brien the bookbinder and the women in the second-hand bookshop Slightly Foxed. They're people with the vision, integrity and honesty to persevere in the face of indifference from the rest of the town. I love the idea of being part of that.

When I went to see the Loan & Mercantile building I knew that I could make something work there, and that my experience and my name might be able to help to get the precinct off the ground. I could not say I wouldn't do it. It would have been wrong of me not to use my experience to do that for the precinct — and what an opportunity I've been given to throw myself into all the history and heritage.

I remember when Oamaru's Natural Heritage Society held organic food and wine festivals in Harbour Street at the turn of this century. The place was alive with music and food stalls and people strolling around, shopping. It could be more or less like that every day in the season if you could just get the people in Oamaru to support it. They don't have to go there themselves, they just have to be proud of it and make sure they tell visitors to spend some time there. I talk to people who come to the restaurant at Moeraki and it's disappointing to hear that more often than not they stayed overnight in Oamaru and were never even told about the old part of town.

I've watched some beautiful businesses struggle and go under because they haven't had the power to attract enough people. Part of the problem is that, generally, people in Oamaru haven't really realised what an opportunity they have to make the town successful. The precinct could be as much of a money-spinner as the bungy jump in Queenstown, the Taieri Gorge railway, the Central Otago rail trail or the goldfields cavalcade.

It's seven months since opening the Loan & Merc in Oamaru. The next step is to use the smaller dining room just off the bar as a fresh fish market and delicatessen selling produce and local wine.

The restaurant is only 50 or so metres away from Oamaru Harbour, where the fishing boats tie up at Holmes Wharf. My plan is to get fish using the same system as in Moeraki — either to use my own quota or buy the fish directly from a commercial fisherman with his own quota. I can see myself going down to the wharf with my little truck, then running a big flag up the pole above the Loan & Mercantile building to let people know we have fresh fish.

As well as running the kitchen, Gilbert handles the delicatessen. He has wonderful charcuterie skills and he makes our bacon, prosciutto, sausages, rillettes, terrines, galantines, pâtés and confits as well as fruit and vegetable chutneys and preserves. He's a natural at all of that. However, it's his ability to control food costs that is his forté. Gilbert makes the restaurant profitable. But you must also have the patronage.

I would never have opened the Loan & Merc if Gilbert hadn't agreed to come in on it with me. We've worked together on and off since 1993, first at Olivers and then at Moeraki. From the time I first met him he has given me faith in whatever it is that I'm doing. He's always been a gypsy though, and he's needed to explore the world. Now he's married Suana, the love of his life, and he's happy to be in Oamaru, working towards the vision.

Whenever I come to town I get a list of what he might need from the countryside to add to his dishes. In mushroom season I detour

LOAN & MERC SLOW-COOKED LAMB SHOULDER AND BEAN HOT POT

Slow cooking gives you the best excuse to seek out these great enamelled iron ovenware pans.

For the beans
1kg white haricot beans (soaked overnight)
2 onions
2 carrots
1 stick celery
1 leek (white part only)
1 bouquet garni
12 whole black peppercorns
6 cloves
1 head of garlic
water to cover

For the meat
2kg trimmed lamb shoulder
1 litre dry white wine
salt and pepper

Method
Cover the beans with water. Bring to the boil then rinse. Add all the other ingredients and cover with fresh water. Cook at low heat for approximately 30 minutes and skim regularly till almost done (the beans will still be firm).

Preheat the oven to 120°C.

Slow braise the meat with the wine in a covered oven dish for 1 hour. Add the beans and cooking juice to the meat. Increase the temperature to 135°C and cook for a further 90 minutes.

Confrérie de la Chaîne des Rôtisseurs

Association Mondiale de la Gastronomie

PROMOTION

Madame Fleur de Lyse R. SULLIVAN

BAILLIAGE NATIONAL DE NOUVELLE ZÉLANDE

Bailliage Régional de Wellington

Nous avons l'honneur de vous faire savoir qu'après examen de votre dossier, nous avons décidé de vous promouvoir au grade de

OFFICIER MAÎTRE RESTAURATEUR

Suivant notre règlement, vous recevrez officiellement, lors d'un prochain Chapitre de votre choix, les insignes de votre nouveau grade.

Nous sommes heureux de vous adresser nos vives félicitations et nos salutations les plus confraternelles.

Fait à Paris, le 11 janvier 2011

Le Président

Siège Mondial
7, rue d'Aumale · 75009 Paris · France
Tél : +33 1 42 81 30 12 · Fax : +33 1 40 16 91 85
chancellerie@chaine-des-rotisseurs.net
www.chaine-des-rotisseurs.net

This French brotherhood celebrates 'the
culture of the table'. The society is made
up of restaurant and hotel owners who
get together to celebrate food.

past the places where I know there'll be field mushrooms, birch boles, slippery jacks and ink caps. I have a friend who drives a bread-delivery truck and he's a real mushroom fiend too. He brings Gilbert all sorts of edible fungi that I wouldn't normally notice. He sits up high in his truck and has a better vantage point to see them than I have in my little truck.

Now that the Loan & Merc is established, there's the matter of managing it. I don't need to be there all the time because I have people there who know what they're doing. I'm around a couple of days a week to keep an eye on the details.

However, if I find the right person to run Fleurs Place at Moeraki — someone with a love of seafood and great ideas about how to showcase it, someone who would put their own mark on the restaurant so that people would embrace it — I'd like nothing better than to be at the Loan & Merc. I'd work as a fishmonger, putting out the signs, making sure everything — the flowers, the walnuts, the fruit and the pumpkins — was placed perfectly. I'd make it look the way I know would attract people to come back again and again and to tell other people about it.

In the meantime my two granddaughters, Flame Callanan-Sullivan and Ruby Sullivan-Doull, are a very handy pair there. Flame is Martin's daughter and Ruby is Kirston's daughter. They're both 21 and they've grown up in my restaurants.

Ever since they were three years old and staying with me at Olivers, their games were always to do with running a restaurant. They'd make their own little docket books and pens, pretending to take people's orders, bringing plates and clearing tables. As they've grown up they've sat at the counter at Olivers and Fleurs Place observing what goes on, and they've both worked in Moeraki during the school holidays. They're both very good baristas and they have the knack for recognising people. They understand how money is made and that a restaurant can't work unless you get paid for what you present. I see the possibility of those two carrying on the business in the future like the next generation of restaurateurs in New Zealand.

But the girls tell me that being my granddaughters is a roller-coaster ride. I heard Flame talking to someone a while ago who said to her, 'It must be lovely having a grandma like Fleur.' Flame replied, 'Yeah, you're seven years old and your grandma pushes you through the fence wires into a paddock full of deer and she's saying, "Run and get those mushrooms! Run! Run! The deer won't hurt you."'

They laugh about it but having me for a grandma can cause some strife with other staff members. I have said to the girls on occasion, 'You know the game, play the game.' One day Flame said, 'But Grandma, it's your game, not my game.' I think they're

Me with chef Gilbert (standing), and
granddaughters Ruby (left) and Flame (right).

getting the hang of it and maybe they'll be all the better for the fact that it's often hard for them.

They're like me in terms of their dedication, industry knowledge and commitment. They were both ready to go off travelling when I opened the Loan & Merc but they decided they wanted to have the excitement of working there. Both loved the building and the concept of the restaurant, and had known Gilbert all of their lives. Both of them from birth till their late teens were vegans. I was 26 when I opened Dunstan House and at 21 they're way ahead of where I was then.

So. I'm an 'ageing' woman with two restaurants on my hands. No matter what happens to Fleurs Place, the Loan & Merc will stand on its own. It's going to be there forever and I won't be. Flame and Ruby are handling it well at present and both Gilbert and I are still agile, healthy and energetic. We are bursting with enthusiasm for what the restaurant, and the historic precinct, can achieve. We'll keep putting the menus on the table every day. We'll keep simply doing what we've always done — presenting the food and wine of the region, this time in an authentic Victorian setting. The Loan & Merc isn't a normal restaurant; it's a tradition in the making.

'NOW, WHAT'S ON TODAY?' IT'S 7 AM FRIDAY AND I LIE IN BED FOR A MINUTE OR SO BEFORE I OPEN MY EYES. I KNOW FLEURS PLACE IS ALL BUT BOOKED OUT AND WE HAVE A BIG FUNCTION TONIGHT AT THE LOAN & MERC IN OAMARU SO I'LL WANT TO SPEND TIME IN BOTH RESTAURANTS.

10

A DAY IN THE LIFE

I scoot to the bathroom and through the dining room window I glimpse the sun-flooded bay, the boats and the restaurant on the spit. The sea is smooth; the boats will go out and we'll have fresh fish today.

Michael brews the first of our hourly mugs of strong white tea, fixes the eggs for breakfast and flicks on the TV so I can catch up with the outside world. Oh how I miss Paul Henry and Pippa Wetzell!

I whisk the linen serviettes off the clothes horse and spend 10 minutes ironing them for tonight's function at the Loan & Merc, then I pull on my gumboots and step outside to feed the hens. If I forget to wear my gumboots in the morning I'm likely to have the misery of wet feet all day. I usually keep a spare pair of socks in my little truck.

While I feed the chooks I run through in my mind what I need to take for the Loan & Merc function tonight: the linen serviettes, and fresh flowers and foliage for the tables. The chefs in both restaurants want fresh herbs everyday: sage, French tarragon, fennel and rosemary. I gather baskets full from my garden and stop the truck on the way to the restaurant to pick the fennel, wild spinach and garnishes from the hedgerows along the waterfront. One of the holiday residents wants me to cut back her rosemary bushes, so that yields a huge armload of pungently scented branches. I'll take most of it into Oamaru later, along with the bundles of pink, pale green and blue hydrangeas I snip from another friend's garden that will make a couple of big arrangements, and six long boughs of wild apples for the centrepieces. As I clamber up the steep tracks, I wonder, Is this the day I'll have a heart attack and who'll find me?

It's quite interesting going to work these days because there are so many more cars leaving the motels, so many more campervans on the road and boats in the harbour than there were when I first came to Moeraki. When I see these signs of affluence I hear my mother saying, 'Things can't be as bad as they say.'

I park my truck and say a quick 'Good morning' to Wayne Annan, who runs the catering caravan on the edge of the car park. He serves takeaway coffee and light dishes for the early arrivals and overflow customers. Then I do a quick skirt around the building, noting what's still growing in the herb garden and checking the beachfront for litter. I have a quick look around the rubbish bins to make sure they've been emptied. Sometimes they're full from the night before because nobody's taken them to the shed over the road, ready to be collected. Some of my young guys would just stack everything at the back door if I didn't stay on their case. I have no idea who they think takes it away! People take so many photos of our building so no polystyrene or plastic containers left out there, please.

Occasionally we discover a seal or a sea lion resting on the concrete apron out the front or on the grass bank at the back of the restaurant; I look for evidence of their visit that needs to be cleaned up. If a seal visits during the day we put a sign outside saying, 'Children and people with dogs: Beware! Seal basking.' Some people don't realise they're wild animals; they're not pets and should never be approached.

After my quick tour of the outside of the restaurant, it's through the back door to the prep room — 'Morena' — and through to the kitchen. 'Morena' because it's 9.30 am and the main contingent's there at 9 am, God willing.

Today's test for all of us comes from a tub of magnificent crayfish. We've lost a chef to a crayfish spike – it's not too long before the telltale red line up his arm means a trip off to A & E in Oamaru. I've sat in A & E with all nationalities of chefs over the years.

I phone the chef from A & E and we decide that the new kitchenhand who's been doing the dishes will have to help out with the prep today, while the gun prep kid moves up one and helps out in the kitchen. In the room at the back of the kitchen, we've got two or three people prepping all day. The chef makes sure they're on task with the cleaning and maintenance schedule, sorting out the fridges, defrosting freezers, wiping and cleaning as well as prepping food. Today some of that might have to be rescheduled and we'll have to get the waitresses to help with the dishes. All of this means we'll need a break during the afternoon, with no meals being prepared while we catch up. And I'll have to find a dishwasher for the next couple of days.

I talk to the chef and the waitresses about the changes on the menu, get all the waiting staff to taste the new sauces and redo the blackboard and computer on the till.

One of my two main front-of-house staff, Deb Duncan, has loaded up the old coal range with pine cones and hardwood, and filled the big galvanised buckets with enough wood to get us through the first few hours. Kelly Gillan, has cleared the answering machine and checked the email for bookings — 30 today — comments and complaints, so I sit down at the little table beside the bar and go over the table plan for the day.

I'm always focused when I do my table plan. It's kept up to the minute so that on a day like today when we're really busy we can keep it under control. I always have a chart in my reservations book so I know how many tables are available at any time. Deb is usually way ahead of me.

The freshly baked scones come out of the kitchen on a tray and away to the caravan. I ring one of the women in the village to ask if her son is coming home from boarding school this weekend. Might he be willing to work for two days washing dishes? She'll ask him. Then it's 10.30 am and a middle-aged man pops his head around the door and says, 'You open yet?' I invite him and his wife in, we start talking and I realise I'm a goner as far as doing much more admin is concerned.

This couple have driven up from Invercargill on their way to Christchurch to help their daughter move out of her earthquake-damaged house; she's been waiting for her insurance claims to be processed but it's all taking too long so she's leaving the city, at least for the time being. We talk earthquakes for a while before I take them to their table. They are the first of a steady influx of diners and by 1 pm the restaurant is nearly full.

Kelly takes a call and passes the phone to me. A lovely lady from Milton says she wants to come by tomorrow with a canteen of bone-handled knives and silver-plated forks that no one in her family wants. Would I like them for the restaurants? Would I ever! We'll decide on a price once I've seen them.

Today is a bonanza because the next call is from the Salvation Army op shop in Oamaru. The woman says a box of mismatched Temuka pottery has just been delivered; if I can't get in today they'll hold it until I call by next week. They know I collect the big bowls and casserole dishes which are perfect for Gilbert's colonial goose dish at the Loan & Merc. Part of the fun of the food is what it's presented on. When we make Cullen skink, we use some of the beautiful old bowls that remain from people's dinner sets. The vegetable dishes weren't used as often as the plates and are more likely to be in one piece.

I trawl through op shops, as well as second-hand and antique shops every week. It drives Mike mad, but I can't not do it. The staff in the second-hand shops I usually go to know what I like to collect; they often keep a little treasure trove of dishes and cutlery back for me to look through. I'm always looking for ashets and serving bowls from pre-1950s dinner sets and interesting pieces of cut glass, especially big fruit bowls and old parfait glasses. I like to serve whiskey in the little Peck's Fish Paste tumblers and I still manage to find beautiful old linen table cloths, serviettes and richly coloured velvet and tapestry curtains.

Coming across good square-ended bone-handled knives, silver-plated forks and soup spoons is always a delight. When the silver gets tarnished from the egg in the whitebait omelettes, we silver dip them and put the forks and spoons though the dishwasher. The bone-handled knives have to be washed by hand because they go yellow in hot water. I've worked out a way to hand-wash them hygienically because we have to meet health department regulations. A lot of my dishwashers think I won't notice if they don't do it right, but I do. I have to explain to them that the knives with the lovely white bone handles cost a lot more than the ones that are slightly yellow. But in a little seafood restaurant or in the big old Loan & Mercantile building you can probably get away with it.

Meanwhile, every table in the restaurant is now full, including those outside. We've been busy seating everyone, taking orders, talking to them about our fish of the day and carrying plates, while keeping an eye on what's coming out of the kitchen. They are handling the extra workload but the strain is beginning to show; I can hear swearing back there, which doesn't often happen because the kitchen is so close to the bar that customers are likely to hear.

Someone at the table of six beside the cast-iron stove is still waiting for his chowder while the rest have already got their first courses so I pick it up from the kitchen. At that moment the phone rings. I answer it because both Deb and Kelly have their hands full and it's someone wanting to make a lunch booking for tomorrow.

A lot of people call right on lunchtime or dinnertime to make their bookings. They'll be eating their lunch and remember that they need to make their lunch booking at the restaurant for tomorrow. Or when they're eating their dinner at home they'll think, 'Oh, better make next week's dinner booking.' We don't have a spare person to answer the phone but I can't say, 'What are you ringing at this time for? Don't you know it's lunchtime?' so I take the caller's details quickly and politely, marking it on the table plan while balancing the bowl in my left hand.

Now there's another ruckus in the kitchen. The head chef, while making the caper and lime sauce, has reached for his bottle of pure lime juice and found it gone. Where is it? Who's got it? It can't just have disappeared! Everyone's denying having touched it and in a flash of inspiration I think, 'Maybe Wayne's got it!' I ring him at the caravan, and sure enough, he does. I tell him that it only takes one person not to do what they're meant to do to make the wheels fall off the whole operation. He says, 'Oh well, I didn't use much.' I reply, 'But you can't take the last bottle. You can't not put it back. Everybody has to accept responsibility for the part they have in the whole thing, or the customer suffers.'

There's another lull until a German couple arrive and stand

at the bar for a while. They both order a glass of good Pasquale pinot gris and sip at it while they survey the room. As the couple at the table by the door stand up to leave, the German man waits for them to step towards the bar to pay their bill, then drapes his jacket over the back of one of the chairs while his wife lowers herself into the other.

Kelly hurries out from behind the bar and says, 'I'm sorry but that table is reserved and we don't have any more room this afternoon. We're fully booked.' The man is not pleased. 'We are here now. No one else is here. The table is empty. We will sit here.'

Kelly points to the words written in chalk on the corner of the table. 'This table is booked all day and most of the evening. We need to clean the table and re-set it for the people coming at 2 pm. I'm very sorry but I can't allow you to sit here.'

Naturally I hear this from the other side of the room and stride over to call Kelly off. I know he's only doing his job and we can't let them have the table but he needs to be a bit more diplomatic. People can be very determined and I expect the Germans to argue with me because in Europe they don't usually have to book; they just wait for the next table.

I approach the couple and say, 'I'm so sorry you've come all this way and we don't have a table for you. It isn't always this busy but today, as you can see, all the tables are already booked. If you like we can seat you on the stools at the corner of the bar or I can ring our restaurant in Oamaru and make a booking for you there.' They are very put out but finally agree to leave the table and drive in to the Loan & Merc.

By 2.45 pm the restaurant is still more than half full but I need to get to Oamaru and back again because we have a full house tonight with people booked in from 5.30 pm and three sittings on some tables. I have been refusing late-afternoon bookings since first thing this morning so that we can take a break for an hour while we catch up in the kitchen. The wait staff will need a break at about 3.30 pm too; they've been running all afternoon because one or other of them has been rostered on dishes and now they need to take time to have their lunch.

We all look forward to our mystery staff lunch and enjoy the chance to sit together.

The boys in the prep room and some of the kitchen staff just graze all day. They're often skinny wee things when they come to work for me, but when they leave they weigh about 100 kg. They're in and out of the huge fridges all day long with their mouths full. The front-of-house staff have much more difficulty finding time to eat and drink. Deb, the thinnest, fastest girl in the west, brings her own snacks and she nibbles away all day.

We put together a staff meal at about 3.30 pm each day. We always have a lovely salad with maybe a roulade, mini pizzas, lots of spaghetti Bolognaise-style dishes or roast pork. I buy a whole pig and we use the belly flaps for the bacon we make in-house, and the rolled pieces of pork or ham steaks with beautiful root vegetable rosti for staff meals. Occasionally we'll have one of Paaka's boil-ups.

It's 3 pm, and I really need to get into town to help set up for tonight's function. We're using the big room out the back for a silver wedding anniversary with 230 guests. Gilbert and his team have everything under control but I need to make sure the room is looking the way I want. I ring Gilbert to see what he needs me to bring in addition to the list he gave me yesterday: a five-litre container of moki for his escabeche, the linen serviettes and the herbs, flowers and foliage I collected this morning.

At 3.30 pm I arrive at the Loan & Merc and deliver the produce to Gilbert. We discuss the details of tonight's menu, which is a degustation plate of cured meats, smoked salmon feuillete, pâtés, vegetable terrines, grilled medallions of beef, daikon cake, boiled duck eggs, manuka-smoked hen's eggs and various pickles, plus the full carvery with a haunch of venison, crispy-skin pork belly, rare roast sirloin, vegetables and salad. For dessert the anniversary couple have chosen comfort food — a brioche and a baked heritage apple stuffed with fruit mince, which has its top and stalk sitting on top to make it look like the perfect apple.

I make two huge arrangements of hydrangeas and foliage for the sideboards, trail apple boughs across the tables and leave the waitresses to set the cutlery, arrange the linen serviettes and stack the plates. There's a full complement of capable staff so there are no problems. I notice three empty cardboard boxes in a corner of the room and ask the girls to get rid of them, saying, 'It's not a storeroom!'

In the kitchen at the Loan & Merc with
Gilbert Prevost.

Mike Hood providing the live
music at Fleurs Place.

It's 4 pm, and while I'm worried and I really want to be there, I need to be at Moeraki. When I arrive half an hour later I see we've had a change of staff, the bathrooms have been cleaned, Deb has cleared the telephone and email messages so there are no dramas there but we've run out of fresh Bluff oysters so I have to change the blackboard so no trace is left that we ever had oysters — it's human nature to want what we haven't got!

A girl who started not long ago is sweeping the floor when a couple comes to the door and, because I'm standing on a chair making the menu change, I'm not quick enough to stop her from saying, 'I'm sorry, we're closed.'

I can't stand it. I've told Kelly not to let her speak to the customers because she looks at them with a blank face and sends them away. I zoom over because I'm always on guard for this type of thing. I have a talk to them, explaining that we can't give them a meal right now. I take them upstairs and give them some bread and dips with a bottle of wine and tell them to look at the ocean and boats in the harbour until service begins.

It's these small things that can make or break your reputation. If you don't stay on guard all the time, you can become like any nameless restaurant. These people had driven from Balclutha to Moeraki over a road that's crumbling into the sea. You know it's not a spur-of-the-moment decision, then to be met by someone who just says 'Sorry, we're closed.' Success doesn't happen by chance. This restaurant is successful because of hard work and constant vigilance.

The first hour or so of the evening service goes smoothly with people arriving and chatting, commenting on the ambience, enjoying the food and Mike's singing. I always talk to as many people as I can and the table plan is working as it should. Then the people for the table of 10 walk in the door. There are only four of them. They're all talking at once, apologising and explaining that there's been a big mix-up and the other six who were meant to join them won't be able to make it. I smile and listen to what they have to say and assure them it's not a problem. I don't mention that we could have put another 10 on this table that we've had to create by joining three tables, and that we've turned six people away.

You can't let it show on your face but with the availability of cellphones, why didn't they give us even half an hour's warning? That's the really frustrating part, and unfortunately it's not a rare occurrence.

There are no further dramas, thank God. People are talking and laughing as they leave the restaurant, promising to come back when they're in the area again, and I usually give them a hug because it always feels as if I'm saying goodbye to guests in my house.

Tonight everyone has gone by 11.30 pm. Unless they're staying in one of the motels or guest houses they have to drive quite a distance to get home. On a quieter night, the restaurant might have emptied by 10.30 pm.

Now we get underway with all the cleaning up and shutting down we need to do before we can leave. Throughout the day we've been putting towels and cloths through the washing machine and we set up several clothes horses in the restaurant to dry them overnight. We use a tremendous number of big towels for the kitchen. Dealing with fish creates a lot of washing. Even though the cleaner will come in first thing tomorrow, we need to mop the floors, clean the coffee machine, scrub the tables, put the chairs up and do the till. Then we check the fridges are locked, especially the outside one, as well as the beer chillers and the red wine stores.

It's time to wind down. Everybody has a staff drink at the end of their shift; make mine a gin and tonic. We sit and talk, dissecting the disasters and I congratulate everyone on pulling together on a difficult day. I love my work and I especially like this part of the day with the gossip, banter and general camaraderie.

We are closed on Mondays and Tuesdays, so if this were a Sunday night some of the staff might decide to go to one of their houses and play cards till 3 am, and I might give them a five-litre tub of lamb shanks to take with them. But there's work again tomorrow and we need what passes for an early night in the hospitality industry.

Now it's just after midnight. We have a routine for leaving the building. At least one other person does the final lock-up with me and we stay to make sure that each other's car starts. Nobody ever drives off without the other one, as a broken-down car will leave you stranded for the night. Thank God for cellphones.

I drive home, make a cup of tea, maybe have some Vegemite on toast and put the TV on. It's usually about 1.30 am when I go to bed. It's a long day but I don't get tired. I'm used to it, and I always have plenty of energy for tomorrow.

IT'S A GOOD LIFE
AND I'VE HAD A GREAT
RIDE GETTING TO
WHERE I AM TODAY.
I WOULDN'T HAVE
MISSED IT FOR ANY
OTHER POSSIBILITIES
I MIGHT HAVE
PURSUED, AND
I DON'T EVER WANT
TO STOP BUT
PEOPLE OFTEN ASK
ME IF I'M THINKING
OF RETIRING.

POSTSCRIPT

I'm 72 years old as I write this, and I am surprised when I look objectively at myself and realise that this is the first time I've been old. If I look at my life as a branch I can see that I am coming close to the slender little tip at the end and I can't ignore it. Even when I had to face the fact that I had cancer I somehow couldn't imagine not being around and doing the things I love.

Now, for the first time, I know I can't go on for ever. I'm lucky at my age to be fit and supple and still have a huge amount of energy so I'm not going to think too much about what's waiting for me around that next corner. Retirement is for retiring people and I've never been one of those.

IMAGE CREDITS

CONTRIBUTORS

Nathalie Brown has worked as a bookseller, broadcaster, publicist, oral history compiler and freelance writer.

Since 1982 her arts, travel, heritage, business and lifestyle features have appeared in newspapers and magazines in Australia, the USA and New Zealand. Her documentaries have been broadcast on ABC National Radio in Australia and Radio New Zealand. Her first book, *Capturing Mountains: the Life and Art of Austen Deans*, was published in 2010. She lives in Oamaru.

Aaron McLean shoots people, places and food. In 2010, Aaron was awarded a Golden Ladle for Best Food Photography at the Le Cordon Bleu World Food Media Awards, which globally recognise excellence in food and drink publishing.

Well known for his food, travel and lifestyle photography, Aaron works for many of New Zealand's leading magazines and 2011 sees the release of his fifteenth book. His images have won *Cuisine* magazine MPA awards in the Home & Food category and the Supreme Award for best use of photography. At the 2009 Travcom Travel Media Awards, Aaron was the winner of the Best Series of Travel Images and was Highly Commended in the Photographer of The Year category.

ACKNOWLEDGEMENTS

NATHALIE BROWN, FOR HER CHARM,
HER BLUE EYES, HER PERSISTENCE,
HER EXTREME TOLERANCE AND HER
DEDICATION TO HER VOCATION.

ERINA AND TERRY McLEAN FOR
GIVING US AARON McLEAN.